DESTINY
Is Within You

Overcoming All Obstacles
and Embracing Success

Musa Bako

Please note that Evangelista Media's™ publishing style does not capitalize the name satan and related names. We choose not to acknowledge him, even to the point of violating grammatical rules.

EVANGELISTA MEDIA™ srl
Via Maiella, 1
66020 San Giovanni Teatino (Ch) – Italy

"Changing the World, One Book at a Time."

This book and all other Evangelista Media™ and Destiny Image™ Europe books are available at Christian bookstores and distributors worldwide.

To order products, or for any other correspondence:

EVANGELISTA MEDIA™ srl
Via della Scafa, 29/14
65013 Città Sant'Angelo – Italy
Tel. +39 085 4716623 • Fax: +39 085 9090113
Email: info@evangelistamedia.com
Or reach us on the Internet: www.evangelistamedia.com

ISBN 13: 978-88-97896-27-2
ISBN 13 EBOOK: 978-88-97896-28-9

For Worldwide Distribution, Printed in Italy
1 2 3 4 5 6 / 15 14 13 12

Dedication

I dedicate this book to everyone who desires to discover God's purpose or the reason why he or she is here on earth. I dedicate this book to all those who are committed to achieving success in their area of calling or place of assignment. I dedicate this book to all those who are seeking to impact their generation in a positive way and help change the world around them.

I dedicate this book to all the people around the world who in spite of their background and the challenges they face still believe and are looking to the future for a great destiny. May you achieve great success wherever you are, reach your highest goal, and find genuine fulfillment in all your endeavors.

Acknowledgments

I am thankful to Almighty God for His sufficient grace toward me and for the inspiration to write this book. Thank You, Jesus, Yours is the kingdom, the power, and the glory.

I appreciate my father in the Lord and the General Overseer of The Redeemed Christian Church of God Pastor E.A. Adeboye and his fantastic wife, our mother, Pastor Mrs. Folu Adeboye for their continued spiritual oversight and the roles they play in my life. I am grateful to God for the privilege to serve under you, sir.

I am grateful for the gift of my wife, Eunice Meque Bako, for all the support I enjoy from her in the service of Jesus. Honey, thank you for always being there for me.

I also say a big thank you to Tamara Ng'ambi and Sarah Akpaka who continue to support me in proofreading my manuscript; you two are gifts and very special to me. Thank you.

Thank you also to Dorcas Rheece, Melissa Rangmen, and Jethro Men, my lovely children, for your continued understanding when Dad is spending a lot of time on the computer or had to be away on a ministry trip. I love you loads.

I thank and honor Professor Adewale Adebojo for giving me his hand of fellowship and for his consistent support. A big thank you to Deacon Benson Ikini and his wife, Joyce, for their encouraging support.

I also honor all the men and women of God whose ministry and books have impacted my life over the years and have helped to prepare me for my calling. Only Heaven can measure the impact of your gift in the church and your contribution to humanity.

Finally, I am grateful to all the Redeemed Christian Church of God Victory Assembly members for your prayers and every support you have given me. I am proud of you all!

Contents

Preface

There are two significant truths of life I would like you to grasp as you delve into the pages of this book:

1. Every person is created for a purpose and every individual has a mission here on earth to accomplish something definite. Nobody was created without a specific purpose. Nobody was ever created in this life to be a loser, a burden, or a pest. We all have great destinies within us; we have been endowed with great potential. We are all created as gifts to our world. We all can be blessings. God has no bad intentions toward anybody. We can all accomplish something great; we can all have and enjoy the best of life.

2. We are only able to discover what we were created for when we are connected to God—who is the source of life. Our connection to God enables us to know why we are in this world and how to effectively pursue and achieve our purpose. Knowing God and having a relationship with Him is not just to overcome sin, die, and go to Heaven; that was certainly not Jesus' primary mission to the earth. His primary mission was and is to give everyone who would come to God through Him the power and ability to enjoy living, to succeed, and to fulfill God's purpose for creating them (see John 10:10). Sin came into the equation because we lost our original position with God and came under the dominion of satan. Therefore, when we come into relationship with Jesus, He deals with the sin factor; this makes us free from satan's legal authority to dominate us, and in that

preventing us from enjoying life to its fullest and succeeding in the destiny that we were created to fulfill.

In our relationship with God, He anoints us to achieve our destiny. Every child of God is anointed of God. You are God's anointed. He anointed you so that you can rise above your limitations, above satanic attack, and so you can express His nature in any circumstance. He anointed you to be what He called and ordained you to be on the earth. He anointed you to express His creativity. The anointing means the ability or the enabling power of God. This means that God has empowered you; He has put His ability in you to enable you to succeed wherever you are. In Christ Jesus, you have been empowered to become what God has destined you to be:

> *Now He who establishes us with you in Christ and has anointed us is God, who also has sealed us and given us the Spirit in our hearts as a guarantee* (2 Corinthians 1:21-22).

The desire you have to be successful and to achieve something significant in life is put inside you by God for His own pleasure and purpose. No desire or ambition is evil in itself, except if it is being channeled solely toward the person's gratification, if the end is to satisfy an ego or is destructive to humanity. If that desire is channeled toward God and to help humanity, then it is a noble thing, and it is of God. The quest to achieve great success, to find joy and fulfillment, to be wealthy, have a great marriage, great family, accomplished career, and be influential is a noble quest. However, your achievement in life, your success in any area of life, should not be an end in itself, but a means to fulfilling something God has ordained to be on the earth for humanity and for His glory.

It is of utmost importance that you realize as a child of God that He has raised you up; you are not under. You are blessed. You are to be God's vessel and a channel of blessings. It is also of utmost importance that you appreciate the truth that as a result of your union with God, He has put His abilities in you. This also means that He is going to be giving you specific ideas, desires, visions, dreams, and passions to achieve certain things in life all for His glory. Anything God-given that can rise in your heart is something you can achieve and become.

I believe that you are about to have a life-changing experience with God as you go on this journey with me. You will discover how to channel the potential that you already have and how you can release it to work for you. You cannot afford to fail in your endeavors; through Jesus we have passed from defeat to victory. There is no idea, ambition, or dream that you have that is beyond your reach. There is nothing you can conceive in your heart that is not achievable. As long as you conceive the idea, you can achieve it, because there is an anointing in your life to make it come through. The Bible says:

Now to Him Who, by (in consequence of) the [action of His] power that is at work within us, is able to [carry out His purpose and] do superabundantly, far over and above all that we [dare] ask or think [infinitely beyond our highest prayers, desires, thoughts, hopes, or dreams] (Ephesians 3:20 AMP).

There is so much potential in you that has not yet been fully maximized. You can really do much more than you have done already and can achieve more, too. The anointing on every child of God is the same anointing that Jesus carried; Jesus did not fail. He could not have failed because He had the anointing. You are not designed to fail. The anointing is on your life so you will not fail. I am convinced that as you follow through these chapters you will learn what you ought to do in order to pave the way in the journey toward becoming a successful and an accomplished person.

The world is about to see in you what it has been waiting for.

RESOURCING MEN AND WOMEN WITH TOOLS
TO SUCCEED IN LIFE AND FULFILL THE REASON
FOR WHICH THEY WERE CREATED.

Chapter One

YOU CAN TAKE CONTROL
OF YOUR DESTINY

You Can Take Control of Your Destiny

Then the word of the Lord came to me, saying: "Before I formed you in the womb I knew you; before you were born I sanctified you; I ordained you a prophet to the nations" (Jeremiah 1:4-5).

The first thing to understand is that you are a child of destiny. Destiny means that before you were born, God had determined why you would exist, what you would look like, who your parents would be, how and where you were going to be born, what nationality you would be, what you would become, and what your future would be.

It does not matter how you were conceived. Perhaps your mother was raped and she became pregnant with you, or your parents never married, or you might be a product of an extramarital affair—it does not matter. No matter how you naturally came into this world, before you were conceived, God had ordained your existence and He had planned a great future for you.

Destiny is also about what God has in His mind concerning your future; it means that before you were born, God had planned your life. God has the blueprint of what He desires for the final outcome of your life here on earth. God never begins something before completing it; He completes it before He puts it into existence. Before you were born, God had finished every work about you (see Eph. 1:4-5).

There are two dimensions to your destiny. The first is exclusively outside of your control, and this includes your conception and how it happened, which family and parents you are going to be born into, your color, race, and nationality. The second is determined by you. You must play a role in your destiny; you can determine whether you will follow God's plan for your life or not, you can determine what future you want to have, either to accept what God's picture is of you or another. You can determine who you want your friends to be, and your spouse; you can determine the career you want and what you want to make of it; and you can determine where in the world you want to live. The fulfillment of what God has in mind concerning your future is largely dependent on you. You did not have any say about your birth, but you have everything to say and do about the final outcome of your life here on earth. Think about it; it's simple. Just as you contributed to where you are today, you are also to determine where you are going to arrive in the future.

YOU DID NOT HAVE ANY SAY ABOUT YOUR BIRTH,
BUT YOU HAVE EVERYTHING TO SAY AND DO ABOUT
THE FINAL OUTCOME OF YOUR LIFE HERE ON EARTH.

Everything that God has planned for you is achievable, but it is crucial that you have a good understanding of what His plan is for your creation. If you do not know it, you may spend all your life trying to be somebody else and not the person God has created you to be—that is a tragedy. I have come to know many people who admire who or what other people are; they admire their color, their chosen profession, the way they walk, their way of dressing, etc., and put a great deal of effort into being like them. But you have got to realize that you are created to be unique—it is in knowing your uniqueness (the real you is how God sees you) and pursuing it that you can find true success, genuine satisfaction, and completeness. When you try to be like other people, or what somebody wants you to be, then you are only going to frustrate the grace of God on your life. The Bible informs us that the grace of God is given to every person according to the measure of the gift of Christ (see Eph. 4:7).

The grace of God is the goodness and mercy of God that is upon a person. It is the ability or enabling power of God in the life of a person, given by God so that person can succeed in life and fulfill the reason he or she was created. This grace of God will work for you as you connect with and work within the gifts and visions that God has of you. It is futile for you to try to be like somebody else simply because you like who they are and what they have accomplished. It is discontenting to try to be like somebody else simply because you were advised that you ought to be like that.

If there is anything you want to invest your life into, it is important that it must be something that you are persuaded in your heart that it is God's original plan for your life. It must be something that will not only make you happy, but make you impact your own generation, make you achieve greatness, and also bring glory to God. When you establish what you are meant to be in life as ordained by God, you must make it your vision, your goal, your passion, and the very reason why you want to be alive or what you live for. Your desires, your visions, and the goals you set for yourself partly contribute to who you are today, and they determine your future.

Destiny Is Within You

Never forget that you are not just existing and surviving through life as a matter of chance. Not one human being is a product of chance. Nobody was created by God accidentally; nobody was created empty and having nothing to offer; and nobody was created useless and a waste of space. It is important to note that everything that God created, including you, is for a specific purpose; you have a purpose in creation and have been designed and endowed with resources to benefit humanity. There is so much that you contain that is yet to be discovered. You are a genius in your own right, created to be your best and with everything you need to succeed in life.

Education does not re-create you; it only brings to life the gifts that are inherent in you. You can achieve destiny, but it is critical that you know what God has planned for you. Your understanding of destiny will invigorate your strength when you need to keep holding on in challenging times and will be your motivation when your world seems to be turned upside down. When the odds are against you, it is the knowledge of your destiny that will keep you focused and keep you going. Walking in ignorance of who you are meant to be will make you give up too soon or can cause you to go around in circles, wasting time and missing opportunities.

You may not feel like it, but you must accept that there is greatness in you. Actually, there is something special about you, and you must find it, accept it, and invest into it. The understanding of what you are about will also make you a fighter; you become willing to give it your all and go all the way because you believe in the final outcome. People who understand their destiny become visionaries. We all have a past, but people of vision never dwell on the past; to them it is history from which they have learned lessons to help them envision a better future. Vision gives birth to purpose; people with a purpose in life are never satisfied with the present, to them the present is only a passageway into the future. The present situation may be tough, but people of vision never give up hope; they are not quitters, their strength is in what they see ahead that others cannot see. Vision is only in the heart of the visionary, other people may not see or understand what they see, but people of vision are never moved by the opinion of others; to them they are only words and are irrelevant. Visionaries' inspiration is the Word of God, what God has said is what moves them.

What you can see today is what you can become tomorrow. What do you see?

What You See Motivates You

Creating an ideal picture of your tomorrow is what will empower you through your journey to tomorrow. What you can see in tomorrow is what you can become. What do you see? Having a vision does not mean that you are not going to have to face any challenges. You may experience delay, you may encounter opposition, and you might experience attacks from different angles—no matter the obstacles you face, remind yourself of the future you see; and if you can keep your focus unbroken, you are going to reach your destiny. The road may not be smooth, success may not easily come to you, and it is even possible to get fired at work or even fail in an important endeavor, but this should not derail you. You will certainly be tried and tested as you go along. And when the going becomes tough, satan will want to make you stop believing your destiny and going after it; but if you can keep your vision in focus, you will get there (see 2 Cor. 4:1; Phil. 3:13-14; Heb. 12:1-2).

Another thing you must always remember is the fact that other people play crucial roles in helping you achieve your destiny. There are people you will need to look out for and identify as part of your journey to destiny, those who are assigned to you by God as helpers of destiny. When you recognize them as people God sent to help you, stick to them, you need them. God has ordained people to be your helpers, you must find them. The devil will want to separate you from your helpers. He will want you to think you do not need anybody, that you can do it all on your own. But the truth is that there are things that you may never have until somebody gives them to you, there are places you may never go until somebody takes you there, there are things you may never know until somebody shows you, there may be people who are relevant to your destiny that you may never get to meet until somebody introduces you to them. There could be things that you will be able to achieve in one year but that will take others ten years, simply because you have helpers in your life.

A Glimpse into Destiny

It is possible to know to some extent what tomorrow holds for you. God desires that you know what tomorrow holds for you, and He has made a way for you to know it. There are two ways through which you can find out or picture your destiny: 1) from the Scriptures (see Ps. 119:130; James 1:23-25), and 2) from your spirit.

First of all, the Word of God, the Bible, has something to say about everything that touches your life: your marriage, your health, your vocation, your finances, your relationships—everything. The Word of God is a revelation of what God has ordained for you and what He wants you to step into. You need to study it, see yourself in it, and act in the light of it like you know it is so. Start to treat the Word of God like a road map. It is your road map to success. In studying the Word, you need to also develop the act of meditation. God says we should meditate on the Word (see Josh. 1:8, Ps. 1:1-2). Through meditation on the Word, you allow your mind to process it and receive the light and understanding God is releasing through it, for the Bible says the entrance of the Word gives light and understanding (see Ps. 119:130). You create a picture of what God has written about you in your spirit as the light of it through meditation shines in you; once your spirit has received it, it becomes a vision, it becomes what you live and hope to see come to pass in your life.

The second way you can know your destiny is from your spirit: destiny is within you, you were created and born into this life with everything inside you waiting to be discovered, developed, and channeled appropriately. You came forth like a seed with a future inside. Your spirit is like a micro chip or a data base. When God breathed His spirit into you, He actually released everything about your life into you. When you are born again, your spirit reconnects with God and it is quickened or made alive. You are a quickened spirit, and now God's idea can rise in your heart. That is why somebody who is not born again cannot find or enter into the kingdom (the will and purpose) of God (see Job 32:8; Luke 17:21; 1 Cor. 2:9-12; Prov. 4:23). One of the ways your spirit will point you to destiny is by generating passion for something inside you. The Bible says in Philippians 2:13, "for it is God who works in you to will and to act in order to fulfill his good purpose" (NIV). Search your heart; that passion you have within you points to destiny. God is at work inside you. If you can learn to follow your heart, it is unlikely that you will miss it. When believers follow their spirits, they succeed, they don't fail. What your spirit points to may appear physically impossible, but there is no impossibility or limitation with the Holy Spirit and the spirit within you.

However, for you to know for sure that what is in your heart is of the spirit and a pointer to destiny and not of your flesh or misleading zeal, you will need to develop your spirit. To develop your spirit, you need to spend more time in prayer and studying and meditating on the Word of God. You need to develop the attitude of meditation in the Word like God said to do in Joshua 1:8:

> *This Book of the Law shall not depart from your mouth, but you shall meditate in it day and night, that you may observe to do according to all that is written in it. For then you will make your way prosperous, and then you will have good success.*

Meditation on the Word is a way you put the Word into your spirit, and by that you grow your spirit to a level where it can understand and discern the voice of God—where it can easily receive from God and rule over logic. Until your spirit starts to rule over your senses, until you can differentiate the voice of your flesh from the voice of your spirit and you clearly know the voice of the spirit, you are going to get it wrong. If your spirit is not developed, you will follow your lusts and emotional drives and mistakenly take it for the spirit. When you are driven by your emotions, which are unstable and easily swayed, you will follow shadows—and you may end up being mediocre if your passion is not generated by your spirit. For instance, some people feel they are successful because they are progressing at a certain pace; yet they may be running toward destiny when they are meant to be flying.

God can also reveal your future through prophecy. Prophesies are given for direction. However, it is important that you know that in this dispensation, God will not speak to you first through a prophet, because in this dispensation, every child of God is a priest and has direct access to God (see 1 Pet. 2:9). God likes to deal with you directly; He wants you to personally know Him and develop a relationship with Him. God likes to interact with you and walk with you. He will speak to you through prophecy only when He needs to clarify or confirm what He has told you before. He will speak to you about something you have not known or heard before through prophecy, only when He has tried to get across to you directly, He could not get your attention, perhaps you had distractions or you are yet to grow to discern and understand His voice. In this light, the prophecy could trigger something in you.

Many years ago, a young man walked into my office to seek counsel and for me to pray for him; he was wondering why God had failed him. He told me his story, how a certain prophet told him in prophecy that God wanted him to sell everything he had, resign from his job, and invest the money into a certain venture. He said he did not really like the idea, never thought about doing that kind of business before, but went ahead to do what the prophet said anyway because he had respect for the prophet, and also because he did not want to disobey God. But everything went down the drain even though he put his all into it. It is a tragedy to rest your entire life on what you are not persuaded of and follow a path simply because somebody told you to.

Yes God still speaks through prophecy; however, prophecy is never the primary way God will direct or reveal His plan to the new covenant believer. God will first speak through His Word and through the witness of the Holy Spirit that is resident in the believer. All prophecies must line up with the Word and must resonate with your spirit for them to be the word of God to you. If you are not going to nurture and develop your spirit to the level where you can by yourself discern the ways of God, the familiar and lying spirits that are out there will seek to take you off the path to your destiny and will bring to ruin what God has planned for you.

To achieve destiny, you will also need to believe that what you have seen in the Word, have received in your spirit, or have had confirmed to you through prophecy is real, and that it is attainable and not impossible. Nothing that God has shown you is impossible. Whatever you can see, you can achieve; it is beyond you only if you cannot see it (see Rom. 4:17-18). It does not matter where you are right now; the challenges you have now do not have power over your destiny. How you look now or feel at the moment is immaterial; what is important is what God is saying about you and what you believe. You may be stagnant right now, but it is not yet the end of your story. You may not have the right contacts at present; yet despite how things seem, God can still make a way anywhere and anyhow. You may not be in the right location, but He can reorder your steps. You may not have the right qualifications, yet He can bring something out of nothing.

HOW YOU LOOK NOW OR FEEL AT THE MOMENT
IS IMMATERIAL; WHAT IS IMPORTANT IS WHAT GOD
IS SAYING ABOUT YOU AND WHAT YOU BELIEVE.

You may feel like you are not the suitable candidate, but He can make a way for you. The assurance from God for you is that you do not have to be the best or the most qualified, God is the One who qualifies people. If you can accept the testimony of your spirit and follow the Word of God, even the devil cannot stop you. My life story is a testimony of how God, through His Word, can transform people and bring them to that place where they never thought they could reach.

You see, I grew up having a problem speaking; I was a stammerer. While attending secondary school, I joined the debating club to motivate myself; but I did not get to speak for my school in any competition. They did not give me a chance; they did not think I could cope on the stage. But God healed me, and today I speak in churches and conferences around the world. A lot of the people I started out with when I newly gave my life to Jesus never thought I would be where I am today and doing the things that I am doing. I was the least likely person. But I discovered God's plan for me in the Word. I believed it, and by believing, I have a successful ministry. You can overcome obstacles and embrace success, too. Maintain your confidence in the report of the Lord, and you will know in your spirit that there is a new dawn coming your way (see Isa. 53:1).

Your Goals Unveil Your Future

Things do not just happen to people; people make things happen. We have to intentionally define what we desire in life, and go for it like our lives depend on it to make it happen. If you aim for nothing, you are always going to get what you aim for—nothing. The higher and more challenging your goals, the higher and sweeter the achievements will be. As such, you will need to know what you want to achieve in life and set goals and draw out plans about how to reach them.

Your goals should be geared toward what you believe your destiny is, and you must also act on your plans. Set a target and walk toward it. You need to ask God what exactly you should do; but do not just sit down and fold your hands and wish that something magical will take place and suddenly it will happen for you. Also note that it is possible you are not going to have a smooth ride on the way toward your destiny; life is full of battles. In order to achieve something meaningful, you have got to be a fighter, you have got to keep your focus unbroken, and you have got to be willing to pay the price. Everything of value has a price tag, precious pearls don't come cheap; likewise, great accomplishments are the result of resolve, dedication, hard work, a disciplined lifestyle, sacrifice, and quest.

The road to destiny is not always smooth and straightforward; success may not come easily. Discouragement will attack you, and there will be distractions and oppositions on the road. When the going gets tough, satan, your adversary, will want to make you concentrate on your past or your present circumstances instead of your goals. He knows that the moment you shift your focus from the target, your direction will change and your zeal for your goals will wane. However, if he cannot distract you or stop you from believing your destiny and going after it—if you can keep the vision in focus, you will get there. Satan cannot stop you (see 2 Cor. 4:18; Phil. 3:13-14; Heb. 12:1-2).

Remember the boy Joseph in the Bible? God told him in a dream that he was going to become a great leader of his people. When his brothers heard it, they became jealous and sought to kill him; instead, they sold him as a slave to men traveling to Egypt. In Egypt, Joseph was put in prison for a crime he did not commit. However, because he trusted God and held on, he eventually became a prime minister in the land where he was a captive. Satan tried but he could not stop Joseph because he could not kill the vision he had of himself.

Determination Is the Key

Having a clear goal—knowing exactly what you want to achieve in life—combined with the will to do what it takes to achieve it is the recipe for a winner. You must have a definite goal to be an achiever.

Success is not a game of luck; it is born out of a decision and being disciplined in character. I have met many young people who do not have a clue about what they would like to become in life. They only wish and pray that something good will happen to them, but they don't do anything definite to make it happen and don't fight for anything. Some people, when asked what they would like to see themselves achieving or becoming in the next ten years, say, "I don't know, whatever." Whatever? That response is tragic. You see, where there is no vision the Bible says the people perish (see Prov. 29:18 King James Version).

It is your dream that paints the picture of your future for you. You are able to live for the future and not be moved by what is going on now only when you know what the future is about. It is the dream that you have that will motivate you and empower you to pay the price. Your dream is your belief system; your dream is what influences your behavior—you can never be bigger than your dream.

Your dream needs your determination to mature and come through for you. You are not going to achieve any significant accomplishment without the fighter in you coming out. Having the determination to achieve anything meaningful in life is triggered by the conviction or belief that it is possible—not easy, but possible. The Bible says to those who believe that everything is possible (see Mark 9:23). You must believe in your God; you must believe in yourself and in your potentials. You must believe you have what it takes to make it happen and it is only a matter of time and it will.

We know that destiny won't arrive in one day, so we are not going to achieve our goals in one day; there will be a space of time between now and then. Also, we know that between now and when we will arrive at destiny, things will sometimes not go as we plan. Things will sometimes appear as tough and impossible. But no matter what happens, we must maintain our confidence in the Lord, and we must set our minds and focus on the place we believe is God's destiny for us.

No matter what, do not allow satan to make you accept the present circumstance as your fate. That is not where you belong; there is no such thing as fate in God's scheme of things. Look through history and you will see that the people who have ever achieved anything significant and impacted their generation were those who showed courage and determination in the face of every odd. If you can stay the course and keep holding on and going on, it's only a matter of time until what God says will happen will happen.

Accepting Defeat Is Not an Option

In pursuit of our destiny, we sometimes hit our target the first time, but sometimes we fail and need to try again. Sometimes we need to try again more than once. Sometimes we need to make a fresh start in order to break through and make headway. Starting all over is not a sign of defeat but of courage and appreciation of one's purpose. To make a fresh start is sometimes needful in order to regain control. Making a fresh start simply means you are back where you were before, with a new chance to start all over again. It is a new opportunity to do what you have done before in a different way. It could also mean the start of something new, something you have never experienced before.

Never forget that to make a fresh start is not a sign of failure but a sign of courage and determination. Sometimes we need to make a fresh start and do something we have done before in a different way to get to where God wants to take us. In making a fresh start, you will need a desire for something better, bigger, and higher. You need to be willing to make a change in some things. If you do not see the need to make a change, if you are simply happy and content with where you are, nothing is going to change. You have the capacity to achieve more than you already have. What people think of you does not matter. Irrespective of your experience or past, you have to put what is past behind you and be willing to start again. You must always make a bold step of faith forward. God may be leading you to take a step of faith to do something you have never done before, something that might appear crazy—go ahead, make that crazy move. God may be telling you to further your education, to start your own business, leave town, or even go into the ministry full time. Take that leap of faith and do as He says. You might find that until you start to make a move into the unknown, you might never make meaningful progress.

Everybody Needs Somebody

As mentioned earlier, you must be aware that there are people assigned to you in destiny; these are your helpers. You will need to find these people. Some helpers may be people who have gone ahead of you on the same road you are taking, they have experienced and conquered the very things you might be struggling with right now. You can learn a lot from their experiences. There are people out there who are blessed, empowered, and assigned by God to inspire you, to encourage and get you through situations in life. It is your duty to find these people. There are people of like passions, people who have been tested and proven, people who have been through the summer and winter and are still standing with God. God will bring them your way, and when you find them, stick with them. Make them your close associates and be ready to learn from them.

There are people you must learn from: you need a father figure and a mentor—helpers. I have seen people push away their helpers; I have seen people walk out on their helpers. When they do, these people find life tougher than it needs to be.

You may, at times, quarrel with people you care about, but because he or she is a helper toward reaching your destiny, you must learn to make up and stick with them: otherwise, you will ruin what you have together and may have to spend ten years on what you could achieve in one year.

In addition to acknowledging the importance of your helpers, you also need to be aware of vision stealers: these are people who do not give regard to what you believe about yourself. Keep away from them, for if you stick with them, they will eventually wear you out (see Prov. 13:20; 1 Cor. 15:33). Keep away from all those who have no respect for your dreams and aspirations. If you stay with them, they will kill your fire and your enthusiasm. Do not get close to anybody who is confessing negative things about what you are doing, who despises what you believe God is making out of you, and who always has a dozen and one reasons why what you are doing will not succeed.

Vision stealers are those people who want to do everything to make you feel less, and they want to put out your fire. It does not matter what anybody feels or thinks about you, and it does not matter what they say, you need to keep confessing what you believe your destiny to be—no matter the circumstances. What you say about yourself, about your future, and even about the people who have got something to do with your destiny must always line up with what God has shown you.

Be careful not to bring down what you are trying to build up—choose your words carefully (see Ps. 34:12-14; Prov. 12:18, 18:21). Don't use your mouth to run down the people God has given you. How you address people shows your value for them. How you speak to them can keep them close and loyal—or send them packing. There is power in your tongue: power to bless and the power to destroy. Your words can also limit you. Don't release a curse on what you are seeking to achieve by saying something that will stop your progress.

Things Will Come Together

When your season is upon you, things will come together. You must realize that your destiny will mature and manifest in an appointed time. God has appointed times and seasons for everything under the sun (see Eccles. 3:1,14; Heb. 2:2-3). You don't create the season, God does. To reach your destiny, you will need to wait for your season. I have seen many people become impatient and step out before their time, and they get into trouble. There is the possibility that what you expect to see may not materialize at the time you expect it to; if that is where you are, neither be discouraged nor start to think and speak as though you no longer hold the conviction that what you once believed to be God's will for you still is. You need to keep trusting, keep waiting, and keep expecting. God's word is not always "yes" and "no." Sometimes He says "wait"; though your desire may tarry, wait for it and it shall surely speak (see Hab. 2:3).

God does not say "yes" and then change His mind soon after. However, there are times when He requires you to wait. For instance, after Abraham received the promise from God, he had to wait twenty-five years for the birth of Isaac (see Gen. 12:1-4, 21:1-5). Joseph received his dream of becoming a leader when he was between 15-19 years of age, yet he didn't become prime minister until he was between 30-35 years of age. David was between 15-17 when he was anointed by Samuel the prophet to be king over Israel, but he didn't become king until the age of 30, and then reigned for 40 years. When you have to wait for something, it is needful; the waiting period is to prepare and equip you for it, to get the place ready for you before you arrive there, or to get the people you are going to be dealing with ready to receive you. Delay is not necessarily denial. If you can wait, and keep waiting, your destiny will break forth like the sun in its strength at the dawn.

Chapter Two

LIVING A POSITIVE, PURPOSEFUL, AND FRUITFUL LIFE

Living a Positive, Purposeful, and Fruitful Life

Look carefully then how you walk! Live purposefully and worthily and accurately, not as the unwise and witless, but as wise (sensible, intelligent people), making the very most of the time [buying up each opportunity], because the days are evil (Ephesians 5:15-16 AMP).

Everybody wants to be happy in life. Everybody wants to be successful in life. Everybody wants to have a great future. Everybody wants to be a blessing and not a burden to people. Everybody wants to leave a good legacy behind.

Not many are happy with mediocrity and failure. Nobody wants a life of struggles and pain—but as the saying goes, if wishes were horses, beggars will ride. As I have said before, we can control much of our own well-being and what we can become in life. To achieve the best of life, we need to be positive and understand our purpose for living. To be a positive and purposeful person, the first thing we need to deal with is what we think about ourselves.

What do you believe about yourself? What you believe about yourself is entirely up to you. You have the capacity to believe whatever you want. You can believe God or believe the lies of the devil. You can believe the Word of God or believe what people have said. What you believe about yourself will have an impact on your worldview, your self-worth, and your personality. Your opinion of yourself can affect the quality of your relationships, your performance in the things you do, and the height you are going to aim at or reach in life.

————————◦————————

WHAT YOU BELIEVE ABOUT YOURSELF IMPACTS YOUR
WORLDVIEW, YOUR SELF-WORTH, AND YOUR PERSONALITY.

————————◦————————

Some people's opinion about themselves is based on what their parents, teachers, friends, or partners have told them. You must never allow people's opinion to define you. They can put a limitation on you and stand in the way of your destiny. You must never forget that it's not what people think of you that counts, it is what you believe or are convinced about—and most of all what God thinks of you. For example, it was told that Winston Churchill, the distinguished World War II British prime minister did poorly in school and failed his entrance exam to the British Royal Military College twice; he was defeated in his first attempt to serve as a member of parliament, but eventually became prime minister at age 62. He later wrote, "Never give in— never, never, never, never, in nothing great or small, large or petty, never give in except to convictions of honour and good sense."[1]

Also, it was recorded that Albert Einstein, the brilliant scientist, did not start to speak until he was 3 years of age and was still not fluent at age 9. Hans Albert Einstein, Albert Einstein's son, reported that his father said one of his teachers described him as "mentally slow, unsociable and drift forever in foolish dream."[2] However, Albert Einstein went on to develop the theory of general relativity in physics and is today regarded as the father of modern physics. In 1921 he received the Nobel prize for physics. Both Churchill and Einstein would not have risen to any place of prominence or significance if they had allowed what was said about them to define their future or decide the perimeter in which they were going to operate. If you refuse to let anybody but God define your future, you too can achieve great success irrespective of your present situation or what was said about you in the past.

Some people's opinion about themselves is based upon past events. In most cases, rape and abuse victims have the tendency to blame themselves for what happened to them, believing that they caused it to happen or deserved it; and as a result, they think they are no good. Also, people who come from abusive backgrounds tend to have low self-worth, and that can impact on their relationships. The fundamental traits of abuse syndrome—what I call a disease for people who have been abused, molested, or taken advantage of—are low self-worth, self-blame, aggression, and lack of trust.

Your past impacts your worldview, your opinion of yourself, and helps form your behavior. Your past can make you see your present in a negative way if not put in proper perspective. People who have not succeeded in the past tend to think they are failures, which can affect their confidence. For example, a person who experienced a failed marriage. Due to the person's past experience in marriage relationship, the person may think he or she is not good enough for marriage or that a future marriage will also fail. A woman who has endured consistent miscarriages may feel cursed or unfortunate, especially if she is from an African, Asian, or other culture that believes in spirits and curses.

However, no matter where you are right now, no matter what you have been through or are experiencing right now, and no matter what was said about you in the past, it does not matter who said what—never forget that God has a picture of you and the reality of who you are is the picture that God has of you. People's opinions and your experiences in life cannot paint over that picture. God is still intending to bring the picture He has of you into reality, but it is what you believe and accept about yourself that can either release you into it or limit it. What you accept is what you will become. The Scriptures say:

> *Finally, brethren, whatever things are true, whatever things are noble, whatever things are just, whatever things are pure, whatever things are lovely, whatever things are of good report, if there is any virtue and if there is anything praiseworthy—meditate on these things* (Philippians 4:8).

People can, and have the right to, think what they want to think about you. People can say what they want to say about you, but what you allow to have power over you is in your control. Know what God is saying about you. Focus on what you want your life to be like and not what you are right now. Make it a personal decision to enjoy every day no matter what happens. Do not be moved by whatever you hear, and do not allow other's opinions to depress you or put any limitation on you. Always remember that you may not be able to change people's opinion about you, but you can prove them wrong. Your achievements will prove them wrong. There is a better day ahead of you. To achieve that, you have got to be resolute. You have got to stay positive, and you have got to be bold and daring. People may attack you, but let it be only because they are jealous of you and not because you are lazy, unfocused, unkempt, or disorganized. Stay positive in the midst of all opposition, tough times, and any trials.

Your Attitude

Your attitude, your approach to life and behavior, determines your future. You must see to it that you are living a lifestyle that is in correlation with where you are going. You cannot behave any which way and have the desired result. Everything that you want in the future requires a certain lifestyle to achieve. You have got to have a lifestyle befitting somebody who wants to reach that future you dream of. It is like people saying they want to be healthy and control their weight, yet their meals predominantly consist of chips, pizza, chocolate, and hamburgers, and they do not do any physical exercise. That is not the lifestyle of somebody who is seriously seeking to be healthy.

We are created as seeds. If a good seed is sown in good ground and watered with God's blessing, it will always yield good fruit. On the other hand, if you sow a good seed in a bad ground, it will yield bad results. That is to say, no matter your destiny, no matter your understanding of your purpose, your behavior will determine what results you will have in life (see Matt. 13:20-22; Prov. 10:4, 22:29).

You may need to ask yourself again, what do I really want to achieve in life? Will my lifestyle, as it is now, take me there? What changes, if any, do I need to make to be on the right track? Your decisions count, the choices you make in life count, the choices you make define what you become. Our God puts it this way:

> *I call heaven and earth to witness this day against you that I have set before you life and death, the blessings and the curses;*

therefore choose life, that you and your descendants may live (Deuteronomy 30:19 AMP).

The things about humankind that differentiates us from every other creation of God is the fact that God created us in His own image: to be a god, and to have dominion over all the things He has made—and God put the power in us to choose or decide our own destiny. This power is called free will. Animals are not created with free will, they are led by instinct and they are not rational, logical-thinking beings. God did all the thinking for them. Instinct is behavior in response to certain stimuli.

God did not make humankind to be led by instinct, we are spirit beings with a conscience to lead us. Conscience is the voice of our spirit and the voice of wisdom. Humankind has a rational personality, created with the power of choice; we can choose our paths in life and how we navigate them. In God's creation of humankind, He also made us to have a desire and ability to walk by knowledge, understanding, and wisdom. The level of knowledge, understanding, and wisdom that a person possesses determines not only the quality of his or her decisions in life but also the level of success. We are able to acquire much knowledge and by it we can dominate and rule over our environment; we can achieve great exploits and create the destiny we choose for ourselves. By reason of increased knowledge, humankind has been able to dominate and subdue the world, exercise dominion over other creatures of God, explore the galaxies, and put men on the moon.

Understanding Gives Life to Knowledge

Knowledge is pivotal for us; without it, we are weak, limited, and ineffective. The Bible says people are destroyed for lack of knowledge; and when you reject knowledge, even God can't help you (see Hosea 4:6). We need knowledge to exist. Knowledge is the collection of information, and correct information leads to a good and productive life. Nobody should make an important decision or life-changing choice without having all the information available. The highest form of knowledge is being equipped with information from God. God can and does transmit information to us. You may be highly knowledgeable in the area of academia, yet still fail if you don't have the wisdom of God. I have seen professors, medical doctors, engineers, lawyers, and accountants who have struggled with and failed in the area of relationship, whose businesses have collapsed, who are finding it hard to pay their bills, and who drive old cars—not because they choose to live a simple life, but because life is hard for them. On the other hand, I have also met people who cannot even as much as write their names, yet they have done very well for themselves and achieved great success in life. What makes the difference is the knowledge that God gives to them. The knowledge that comes from God is divine and is superior to worldly knowledge. Divine knowledge such as an idea inspired by God can succeed where worldly knowledge is limited.

Understanding is the correct interpretation of acquired knowledge or the insight one receives regarding how to use the information or what to do with the knowledge acquired. You need understanding before you can move; without understanding, information is a waste. That is why the wise King Solomon said, "in all your getting, get understanding" (Prov. 4:7). Understanding is critical in making the right decision. Paul the apostle admonishes that we pray for God to enlighten our understanding.

> *That the God of our Lord Jesus Christ, the Father of glory, may give to you the spirit of wisdom and revelation in the knowledge of Him, the eyes of your understanding being enlightened; that you may know what is the hope of His calling, what are the riches of the glory of His inheritance in the saints* (Ephesians 1:17-18).

It is understanding that gives life to knowledge, you need to understand the knowledge that you gain. Without understanding, information can be confusing. Without understanding, knowledge stays dormant, it is not empowered to produce, and can actually be destructive if you misinterpret the information. Again, it is understanding that gives life to knowledge; and without it, knowledge is wasted. It is the understanding of what to do with knowledge that leads to wisdom.

Wisdom is the ability to apply knowledge correctly and skillfully. Of the three—knowledge, understanding, and wisdom—wisdom is the chief of them. The Bible says, "Wisdom is the *principal* thing; therefore get wisdom" (Prov. 4:7). Wisdom is principal because it is also the application part of the three. It is immaterial the amount of knowledge and understanding one has acquired if the person does not apply it to his or her life—that person is no different from a foolish person.

Every person needs the operation of wisdom to make healthy and productive decisions. Wisdom develops in us as we increase in understanding—the more we gain understanding, the wiser we become. Furthermore, there is also the perfect wisdom that is from God. The wisdom from God is manifest when we act on what God has shown us to do rather than what we have learned in a classroom or heard on the news.

When you are acting in a particular way based on the understanding you acquire through study, that is wisdom, but is it common sense wisdom? On the other hand, when you are acting in a particular way based on the understanding you have received from God, that is divine wisdom or the wisdom of God. The wisdom of God may not always appear as a clever or wise thing to do, as sometimes the wisdom of God may go contrary to common sense—and definitely it goes against worldly wisdom. However, acting on God's imparted knowledge is pure wisdom and vastly superior to worldly wisdom. Common sense wisdom may have limitations, but on the path of divine wisdom, you won't get it wrong and will never fail.

Common Sense Versus Divine Wisdom

In August 1996, I was transferred to lead a church in Yola, a city in northeast Nigeria. It was a very small congregation. A few weeks after arriving in Yola, I heard the Lord say to me to hand over the pastorate of that church to another person and to move into the center of the city to initiate and lead in the planting of a new church. It did not appear to be a wise thing to do, and many of the people I was working with did not think it was a good idea. Also, my boss, my immediate leader, told me that was not what I should be doing at the time, and I did not have any funding.

However, as I followed the voice of God and got something started, God stepped in; and shortly after, a brother came to me and gave me money to use to rent a house for my accommodation. The money was enough to pay rent for two years. At that time, I did not have a house in Yola, I was sharing a place with someone; so I could not bring my family to be with me. When the brother who offered me the money left, I heard God say the money should not be used for my house rent but to use it to fund the new church plant. It really did not make any common sense to me at all. It made more sense to stay in the church in Yola and try to grow it. It made more sense to use the money the brother gave me to get a house, which my family and I desperately needed. I did not understand fully what God was up to, but I simply did what He said to do.

Sometimes the wisdom that is from God contradicts human wisdom. The money for my rent was part of what I used as a down payment for the purchase of the land where the Redeemed Christian Church of God (RCCG) Victory Assembly Yola started. I am glad I followed the voice of God and not common sense; today RCCG Victory Assembly Yola is a dynamic church—one of the largest in northeast Nigeria and is an RCCG regional headquarters church. Also since then, RCCG Victory Assembly Yola has established several other churches and has raised many pastors who are leading churches within Yola and in other cities.

God had a bigger plan than I envisaged; He was using my little seed to create a path to a bigger destiny. Ten months after the start of the new church, God opened a door for me to move to Germany to become the pastor of another RCCG church in Bonn. We must make our choices based on good knowledge and understanding—but it's more important that we choose to follow the way of wisdom, and it is even better when the wisdom is from above. Following the way of God is wisdom; when you go on that path, you will never fail, it will bring you to a place of great success.

Your Choices

You were created with the power of choice; what choices are you making? We all make choices every day. We choose when to get up every morning, we choose what to wear, we choose when to eat and what to eat, and we choose where to go to, what to do, and how to spend our day. The choices we make every day determine what we become. You can choose to live or choose to die. You can choose to be a success or a failure. You can choose to be a winner or a loser. You can choose to live in poverty or aspire to be comfortable and wealthy in life. You can choose to live a happy or a sad life. You can choose to be a person of honor or a person of dishonor. You can choose who you want to marry or live with. You can also choose to live in freedom or be in bondage. You can choose your destiny. The power to choose the outcome of our lives is a gift from God. He created us with that ability and He will not take it away from us. The two trees God put in the Garden of Eden (humankind's first home) were symbols of our gift and power of choice.

People are created with an inherent ability to make choices, and what you choose you become. Although you cannot control what people think of you, you can choose what impact their thinking makes on you. You can choose what you want to be. As such, it does not matter what people think of you as long as you are being obedient to God's Word. Many a time we put the blame for what is happening to us on satan. Sometimes we even blame it on God or other people. We seldom look within ourselves to see what we may be doing that is affecting our progress. With this mentality governing our thinking, we look at the good things that are happening in other people's lives and we make excuses for why things are the way they are in our lives. Sometimes we use the excuse that God did not give us the opportunity He has given others. In other cases, we may find ourselves saying, "Other people are happy and are doing well because they have not confronted satan or evil at the level I have," when yet the actual truth is that there are people who have a similar or worse history to ours and have conquered the odds—they have triumphed in life.

Do not blame your circumstances on others or satan—you are responsible for your own life. If only you can sit down, think about life, make the right decision, and act upon such decisions, things will turn around for you.

We make our choices in different ways, some unconsciously and some consciously. Either way, every choice that we make impacts our lives. An unconscious decision is made without giving much thought to it, not really weighing the implication of the action, and callously or carelessly committing to do or ignoring to do something. This happens when people make light of everything important or become too busy to take time to consider the choice. A lot of times the result is catastrophe and regrets. And when it is too late, the people who acted that way say, "I feel so sad. I wish I had given the decision serious consideration. I did not know it would turn out this way."

A conscious decision is made when people decide on a path with the full understanding of what they intend to do or not do and what the implications of that decision might be. The outcome of this decision can either be a positive one or a negative one. Success comes out of a conscious and positive decision, a decision that is formed based on good knowledge and understanding. In other words, a conscious decision is when you know what you want to do and what you want to have. You know that you are acting on a conscious decision when what you do is based on that decision and when all your actions are measured toward a set goal or target.

For instance, if you want to be saved and have a relationship with God, you need to consciously choose to accept Jesus as your Lord and Savior or alternatively reject Him if you do not desire any form of relationship with Him. If you want to go to Heaven, you have got to choose to be holy, because the Bible says that without holiness no one will see the Lord (see Heb. 12:14). If you want to make friends and keep them, you have to decide to show yourself friendly as the Bible has said and choose to be loyal to friends, too.

If you want to improve your chances of gaining a good and well-paid job and rise steadily in your career, you may make a choice to further your education or be retrained in some way. If you choose to be educated, it is never too late to study; you are choosing to improve the standard or quality of your life. If you do not make this choice, you are settling for the consequences of not having a higher level of education, and the setbacks of not improving your skills will affect your progress.

As such, this choice could mean that you are not equipped for the better chances in life that you could have positioned yourself for.

If you want to be successful and comfortable in life, you will need to overcome laziness and idleness. You need to be willing to take risks; decline government handouts, especially if you are able bodied; be industrious and make yourself marketable—start working today toward having a better life. If you want financial freedom and enlargement, you need to choose to invest for increase. Likewise, if you want to avoid a painful marriage and divorce, then you have to carefully and prayerfully choose the right person to marry—not just choose anybody you meet on the street. You cannot enter into a marriage covenant with intentions of spending the rest of your life with a person you don't know or know so little about. You will also need to decide from day one to be committed and be ready to go all the way through life with this person—no matter what.

You make choices, not just by your decisions made consciously or unconsciuosly, but also by your indecision. Indecision is when a person is between opinions and unable to take a decisive step. Indecision usually happens when people do not know what they really want and cannot take specific measures or actions toward a specific goal. The person who is indecisive is double-minded. Some may call him a man in the valley of indecision. In the valley of indecision, there are no specific goals, no defined targets; and as such, life here goes in a circle, and it is sometimes stagnant, and the person here mortgages his future to chances. By chances I refer to seeing life as a gamble. When people aren't sure of what they really want, they take on everything that comes their way.

You can be easily influenced by people when you are in indecision, and, unfortunately, people, situations, or circumstances will decide for you. You cannot hold on to something and pursue it no matter what because you are not convinced about anything. You do not even know what you really want. You cannot succeed with that mindset. Pray, and then make the best decision possible based on all the information and your correct understanding of it.

Lifestyle Choices

You also make choices through your lifestyle. Your routine or lifestyle forms your character. Your character says who you are and also determines what you are going to attract to yourself or become. For instance, a life of drunkenness and drugs will damage your career, affect relationships, rob you of your finances, and damage your health. If you make a choice to live on drugs and alcohol, you are also choosing the consequences of that lifestyle. A "carefree life," a life lived without values and purpose, means that you take anything that comes your way; you believe in fate. You live with a *que sera sera* attitude—whatever will be will be. When you think that things just "happen," you need to know that nothing will happen. You must determine what should happen and what you give yourself to—the decisions you make determine what you will get or become in life.

A life of sexual immorality means you are choosing to put on the line your health, your marriage, or whatever relationship or future relationship you have or may have. You must realize that you are risking much—maybe even your life—when you choose that lifestyle. You can also choose to live a lazy life; this simply means you are choosing to be at the mercy of charities or certain government support schemes. You may have chosen not to make a difference in life or do anything that will affect or influence your generation positively. This is most unfortunate because by making a choice to live a lazy or immoral lifestyle, you may not rise above mediocre.

When making choices, nothing you do is immaterial. Everything counts toward progression or retrogression. Your attitude, your habits, and your decisions can affect you and what you have acquired so far. Take time to think and make the right choices.

Association Choices

You make choices by your associations, the people with whom you connect or form alliances. These people can impact you whether you know it or not. Knowing the right people to form alliances with and the ones to keep at arm's length is a decision you must make routinely throughout your life. Your associations say much about you, your values, the dreams you have, and how high you want to rise in life. The people you associate with have influence over you in some way; that is why the Bible says, "Do not be deceived: 'bad company corrupts good habits'" (1 Cor. 15:33). It is also often said that he who moves with the wise will be wise.

Please understand that there are people you cannot bond or form deep relationships with because of the negative impact they can have on you. You may have something to do with everybody you come into contact with, but do not be deeply and intimately involved with just anybody. If your close friends or associates are cheats and liars, they are likely to brush off onto you some of what they have. If you hang out with people of immoral thought and behavior, they are likely to pollute your mind. If you enjoy clubbing and meeting with clubbers and you are single, you are likely to marry someone in those same circles; and if you are married, you stand the risk of developing a relationship that can put your marriage in jeopardy.

If you connect with great thinkers, people of high standards in life, people who have a passion for success and live positively, you are likely to start to think highly of yourself and expect great things in life. Your association with great people will stir up greatness in you. You can associate with people in different ways. You can make associations by reading books. Books are powerful ways we connect with the spirit in somebody. People write books to communicate their values, their understanding, and whatever they have in them, with the intention of impacting the readers.

Usually people choose a book because they want to know more about specific subject areas, and those type of books can change lives. There is an unspoken relationship that develops between a reader and the author, and when the reader finds the author's experiences interesting, the book starts to influence the reader's worldview and behavior. That is why not every book should be read, only those you desire to impact you. Books written by Kenneth E. Hagin, E.W. Kenyon, Kenneth and Gloria Copeland, Myles Munroe, and T.D. Jakes have helped release many people into their destiny—including me. You can connect with people by admiring their style and by watching them closely, even from a distance.

Many football stars, singers, and movie stars have become role models to millions of people they have not even met and do not know. When I was a teenager, I had friends who smoked weed (marijuana) and put their hair in dreadlocks because they wanted to be like Bob Marley the reggae singer. We do not have to physically meet somebody before he or she starts to influence us. When people admire others and desire to be like them, an association develops; and as they watch closely and learn more, they start to influence them in some way. For instance, many Michael Jackson's fans dressed and danced like him. In the Christian world, Pastor Kenneth E. Hagin's life and ministry has positively impacted many lives around the world, people he has never met. Only eternity can measure the extent of that impact.

You can also form associations by fellowshipping directly with somebody, which is very powerful. Who are your friends, acquaintances, partners, etc.? Who are the people you have sex with? The Bible says when a man sleeps with a harlot, he becomes one with her (see 1 Cor. 6:16). With whom do you spend much of your time? Who are your counselors and close confidants? They can all help to shape your life and destiny in one way or another.

But there are also people who will stop your progress—you have to disconnect with these people to be able to think straight. Disconnect from these people so you can make a fresh start. Victory Assembly, the church I work with, offers what we call "a drop-in center," which is a lunchtime fellowship for roofless people, the elderly, and people who need the service. Some of the people who come to our drop-in center have problems with substance abuse and addiction. We help them by working with agencies that specialize in these kind of issues. Normally, a patient who has accepted treatment is removed from his or her current environment to a new location to disconnect from detrimental associations. Likewise, there are people who are surrounding you that you have to *disconnect* from to overcome a habit. On the other hand, there are people you need to *connect* with in order to succeed in life. Your values, dreams, and life goals should determine the people to align with and those to keep at arm's length.

———————◁◦▷———————

YOUR WORDS ARE POWERFUL—THEY JUSTIFY OR CONDEMN YOU.

———————◁◦▷———————

You make choices through the words you use. Everything that you see was created with words. God thought of everything that is seen and commanded it into being with words: He simply said, "let there be," and it was so. God created man in His image to be able to function like God, to be a god here on earth and to exercise dominion over all that exists on the earth (see Gen. 1:26-28). One of the fundamental things about man being in the image of God is his ability to declare with words what he desires to be and it becomes so. After the creation of Adam, his first demonstration of his supernatural abilities and influence over the things on earth that God gave him charge over was to name them, and whatever he called them is what they became (see Gen. 2:19). Your words are powerful; they can justify or condemn you. It was Jesus Christ Himself who said, "for by your words you will be justified, and by your words you will be condemned" (Matt. 12:37). What you say has a spirit and can affect you either way. The Bible says that "death and life are in the power of the tongue" (Prov. 18:21). You need to watch what you say about anything that is of any interest to you—your words are powerful.

Do not speak death to your business, nor speak ill health to your body, and you must avoid speaking evil into the lives of your loved ones. Do not declare with your own mouth the future that you do not want to have—rather, declare the future you want to have. You exercise your authority through the words you use. You cannot rise above your confession; your words will either limit you or release you into greatness. It is what you declare that you will become, so you need to start declaring what you want to see happen to you and not what you feel, not what other people are saying about you or your situation, and not what you see—declare what you want to see happen.

You make your choices by what you say. What you say may not take form and materialize in one day, but the moment you release those words, the spirit in those words starts to work in the direction you have spoken.

Endnotes

1. http://www.biography.com/people/winston-churchill-9248164; accessed June 27, 2012. Speech given at the Harrow School, October 29, 1941.

2. http://www.jewishworldreview.com/cols/sowell083001.asp; accessed June 27, 2012; http://www.lucarinfo.com/inspire/deinstein.html; accessed July 7, 2012.

Chapter Three

CHOOSE TO PROSPER AND IMPACT YOUR GENERATION

Choose to Prosper and Impact Your Generation

Prosperity is a choice; nobody was created for a life of misery. If you choose prosperity and follow the path that leads to it, your background or race will be immaterial. The Bible says you can make your way into prosperity:

> *This Book of the Law shall not depart from your mouth, but you shall **meditate** in it day and night, that you may observe to do according to all that is written in it. For then **you will make your way prosperous, and then you will have good success*** (Joshua 1:8).

You can make the way to your dream land, you can overcome the odds, you can make it to your destiny irrespective of your history. There are many successful and influential people living today who did not have fathers at home when they were growing up, their mothers had them out of wedlock, their fathers walked out on them, they did not receive the best care, they did not live in the most ideal neighborhood, they did not attend the best schools. How can this be? Somewhere along life's journey they made a positive choice—they refused to let their history limit them, and through hard work and determination they achieved great success. Movie star Djimon Hounsou and television star Oprah Winfrey are good examples of such success stories.

Djimon Hounsou was born in Cotenou, in the Republic of Benin in West Africa. He was the youngest of five children. At the age of 13, his parents sent him to Lyon, France, to live with his older brother, but he ran away and lived on the streets of Paris. For several years he was homeless, sleeping under bridges, searching garbage cans for food, and begging for money to survive. He did not learn English by attending school, he learned it by watching television. However, Djimon not only went on to become a top male model in Paris, he also landed roles in popular U.S. television programs and in several major movies. He said about himself, "School bored me. Being educated and being intelligent are two different things. I thought I was smart enough. And I wanted to be an entertainer. I stopped going to school as a way of saying I was mature, a way of saying I was going to choose who I was going to become."[1] Today Djimon Hounsou has a net worth of $10 million, and has also become the fourth male African to receive an Oscar nomination for acting.

Oprah Winfrey was born in Mississippi to young, unwed parents. She was raised by her grandmother until she was 6 years old. Oprah then moved to Milwaukee, Wisconsin, to live with her mother and half sister in a boardinghouse. Oprah's mother worked as a maid and sometimes relied on welfare to support the family. Despite her humble upbringing, Oprah Winfrey went on to become a successful businesswoman, transforming herself from a news anchor to a talk-show host and eventually to own her own multiplatform media empire. According to Forbes magazine, she is now worth more than $2.7 billion.[2]

Many people who were born and raised by very poor parents have made choices that pointed them in the direction of their destiny—a life of fulfillment and prosperity. Nobody in their lineage was ever wealthy; their family from generations past was so poor that even poor people called them poor—but today they are company chief executives, directors, business owners, doctors, lawyers, entrepreneurs, great song writers, movie stars, and wealthy athletes. Two other examples of people coming from very poor backgrounds but who made the right choices and ultimately became and are positive influences in their generations are the former U.S. Secretary of State Condoleezza Rice and the current U.S. Supreme Court Justice Clarence Thomas. These people chose the way of God's destiny for their lives and decided to impact their nation and the world.

You can break the family curse; you can end the cycle too. It is all about choices. Joshua 1:8 makes it very clear that we are the ones to make our way to prosperity and success. God does not choose our way for us, He only blesses it. He will show us what to do or which way is better, but the ultimate decision is ours.

You must accept the fact that God is excited to be involved with our well-being and desires that we all experience prosperity; there is no doubt about it. The Bible says in Psalm 35:27:

> *Let them shout for joy and be glad, who favor my righteous cause; and let them say continually, "Let **the Lord** be magnified, who **has pleasure in the prosperity of His servant**."*

Prosperity is not only about having more money, it is also about having fulfillment in our relationships, it is about having a great marriage, it is about having a satisfying profession and rising through the hierarchy, it is about doing well in our studies and achieving success in all we do, it is about our business or investments bringing in dividends, it is about having a healthy life and not being weak and sickly. God desires for us to have healthy lives and live long so we can fulfill His purpose for creating us. Prosperity is about achieving progress in the things you are involved in. Jesus said that we are to occupy till He comes:

> *He said therefore, a certain nobleman went into a far country to receive for himself a kingdom, and to return. And he called his ten servants, and delivered them ten pounds, and said unto them, Occupy till I come* (Luke 19:12-13 King James Version).

To occupy means to take over something, take charge, rule over it, engage it and bring it to a place of profit. We have a mandate to occupy.

The New King James Version says it this way:

> *He [Jesus] said: "A certain nobleman went into a far country to receive for himself a kingdom and to return. So he called ten of his servants, delivered to them ten minas, and said to them, 'Do business till I come.'"*

We have a mandate to lead a profitable life. God wants us to occupy, take charge, and do business wherever He has put us and over whatever He has given to us and to be in a place of influence so we can make a difference. Believers are not meant to be observers wherever we are, we are not meant to be on the periphery of things, we are not meant to be at the receiving end, but the giving end. Believers are to be at the cutting edge. We are called to be life changers, community changers, and city changers.

You need to take your place. We all need to take our places. We need to start occupying, we need to start making a difference and influencing society. We cannot afford to be poor, weak, and isolated. We cannot afford to be unknown and unnoticed. Our voices must be heard and our influence must be seen. People must look up to us for answers and direction. As such, God is counting on us to do just that for Him. We cannot effectively occupy as we should if we are just stalled, stale, poor, defeated, unmotivated, not advancing, and not growing.

To make any impact, we must be seen as effective, fruitful, and advancing in the things that we do. We need to be moving forward, growing, enlarging, making progress, achieving results, and touching lives. You cannot influence anything if you are not being fruitful in the things you do. You cannot influence anybody if you are always receiving and never giving. You must rise to the place of influence. You can be influential only when you are being effective, fruitful, and progressive. When the blessing of God starts to manifest in your life, it will not only make you fruitful, it brings you to that place where you can exercise dominion. God pronounced the blessing on Adam and Eve in order for them to have and exercise dominion. The Bible says:

> Then **God blessed them**, and God said to them, "Be fruitful and multiply; fill the earth and subdue it; have dominion over the fish of the sea, over the birds of the air, and over every living thing that moves on the earth" (Genesis 1:28).

Being blessed is being empowered to succeed, to increase, enlarge, multiply, and become influential. Until these traits start to manifest in your life, your ability to exercise dominion will be very limited. Your voice will not count where it matters; it is for that purpose that God desires that we prosper and multiply. Isaac became a great man such that the Philistines became envious of him, not by reason of who his father was, not by reason of his citizenship, and not by reason of his academic attainment—but by reason of his increase. His increase made him a great man:

> Then **Isaac** *sowed in that land, and reaped in the same year a hundredfold; and the Lord blessed him. The man began to prosper, and continued prospering until he* **became very prosperous;** *for he had possessions of flocks and possessions of herds and a great number of servants. So the Philistines envied him* (Genesis 26:12-14).

True Prosperity

God has promised to prosper you as a result of your covenant with Him. True prosperity comes in covenant with God (see Deut. 8:18). You must believe in prosperity and receive it as your portion so you can dominate lack, sickness, and disease, help take away the pain of poverty and shame from the poor, engage the kingdom of Jesus in order to enlarge it, and allow God to show His manifold wisdom to our generation through you. Psalm 16:6 (NIV) says, "The boundary lines have fallen for me in pleasant places; surely I have a delightful inheritance." We cannot doubt the fact that God desires us to prosper. We know He does, for in Christ Jesus, our inheritance is a delightful one.

The Scripture from Psalm 16:6 is also saying that God has put a boundary between you and any unpleasant situation. You are to prosper and be in good health. The Bible is full of Scriptures about prosperity in its broadest sense, and God has also made grace available for us to achieve it.

However, we have a role to play in achieving prosperity; we are the ones to choose prosperity and make our way toward it. One of the things that can put us on that path is having a covenant relationship with God. You must understand that God is a God of covenant. We come into covenant with Him by accepting Jesus as our Lord and Savior.

If you are born again, you are a covenant child of God. Anybody who has not accepted Jesus as Lord and is not born again has no covenant with God. Anybody who is not saved has no claim on God or the benefits of the kingdom. If you are not born again, you do not have a right to the goodness of God. But you can come into relationship with Jesus today—right now, if you want to.

Just pause a moment and say the following prayer from your heart: "Dear God, I believe in You, I believe that Jesus is Lord, I believe He took on flesh, and for my sins He hung on the cross; He died and paid in full the penalty for my sins. I believe on the third day He rose from the dead for my justification. I receive Jesus right now as my Lord and my Savior. Right now I believe I am saved and my name is written in Your book of life. Thank You, Lord, for my salvation. Amen."

If you prayed the prayer, I encourage you to look for and attend a church where the Bible is taught. Becoming a church member is about fellowshipping with other believers and learning more about your relationship with Jesus, you become established and grow in your faith. You can also contact me at the address found in the back of this book. We will keep you in our thoughts and prayers.

I RECEIVE JESUS RIGHT NOW
AS MY LORD AND MY SAVIOR.

There are many good things that our good God does for both the unsaved and the saved alike, things like making sure you do not go to sleep hungry and keeping you safe when you take a journey. Similar life events happen to everyone every day. A woman does not have to be born again to conceive a child or a man to become a father. God's world was created for all human beings to enjoy; and in His capacity as the Creator and a merciful God, His ultimate desire is for all to come to the saving knowledge and acceptance of His Son as the Redeemer.

But you must know that there are certain interventions by God that can happen to a person only as a result of a covenant relationship with God; such as God answering prayer, taking over and fighting your battles for you, and God supernaturally intervening for you in difficult times. God can bring something out of nothing, He can make a king out of a pauper, He can make the barren flourish, the desert to spring forth life. Where it is hard for other people, He can make it easy and comfortable for a covenant person. He can change laws in favor of a covenant person. He can turn the heart of an enemy of a covenant person and make him a friend.

In the covenant you can walk in and enjoy the supernatural interventions of God and not all achievements will come about because of your effort or hard work but because of God. There are some things of God that a person cannot experience outside the covenant. It is also part of the covenant that, as covenant people, we honor God always, remembering to give Him the glory due His name. We put ourselves on the way toward prosperity when we do that.

We show that we honor God by our lifestyle. God is honored when our lives show respectful fear of God. God feels despised when our lifestyle is not right with Him. The Bible puts it this way in Proverbs 14:2, "He who walks in his uprightness fears the Lord, but he who is perverse in his ways despises Him." If you are not living right and are not showing regard for God in your lifestyle, how can you expect Him to have any regard for you?

We also show regard or honor to God when we acknowledge that what we have are gifts from Him. No matter how wise we are or how hard we work, there are things we can never achieve except by the help of God. We show that recognition by bringing Him offerings from the blessing He releases to us:

> *Give to the Lord, O families of the peoples, give to the Lord glory and strength. Give to the Lord the glory due His name; bring an offering, and come before Him. Oh, worship the Lord in the beauty of holiness!* (1 Chronicles 16:28-29)

There are four fundamental ways through which we give God glory: first, through our offerings. We are to give our first fruits, our tithes, offering of thanksgiving, and pay our vows. Also, in the covenant you will need to make yourself available and useful in the service of God. Being of service to God attracts God's rewards in diverse ways, especially in the area of our own needs:

> *So you shall serve the Lord your God, and He will bless your bread and your water. And I will take sickness away from the midst of you. No one shall suffer miscarriage or be barren in your land; I will fulfill the number of your days* (Exodus 23:25-26).

> *For God is not unjust to forget your work and labor of love which you have shown toward His name, in that you have ministered to the saints, and do minister. And we desire that each one of you show the same diligence to the full assurance of hope until the end, that you do not become sluggish, but imitate those who through faith and patience inherit the promises* (Hebrews 6:10-12).

There is nothing that you will do for God's sake that will be in vain. He will always reward you in return. And in most cases, answers to prayer come as a reward of our service to God (see John 15:16). So no matter how busy you get, you must create time to serve and be faithful, selfless, and fruitful for God. Do not make yourself unprofitable in the kingdom.

Choose a Worry- and Stress-free Life

Worry is a disease. It is not of prosperity, it destroys one's sense of security; it ruins happiness; it can ruin relationships; it can kill your confidence and can cause you unnecessary pain. We understand from Scriptures that we cannot add a single hour to our lives by worrying. Our Lord Jesus puts it this way:

> *Therefore I tell you, do not worry about your life, what you will eat or drink; or about your body, what you will wear. Is not life more important than food, and the body more important than clothes? Can any one of you by worrying add a single hour to your life? So do not worry, saying, "What shall we eat?" or*

"What shall we drink?" or "What shall we wear?" For the pagans run after all these things, and your heavenly Father knows that you need them (Matthew 6:25,27,31-32 NIV).

To live a positive and healthy life, you must know how to live a worry- and stress-free life. Stress is a factor that creates a mental, emotional, or physical strain. It is a state of unresolved tension from the pressures, irritations, and demands of life. Worry is the feeling of anxiety, unhappiness, feeling troubled or uneasy. Some symptoms of stress include mental and emotional fatigue, drug and alcohol dependency, loss of appetite, physical weariness, high blood pressure, frequent headaches, stomach problems, heart problems, migraines, ulcers, insomnia (sleeplessness), and hypertension.

To avoid stress, we need to learn how to leave to God what is not in our power to change, we need to know what is not our assignment and pass on it, we need to learn to say "No" to some requests and not always say "Yes"—even when we want to say yes. Our focus in life must not be about material gains only but rather to fulfill God's purpose here on earth. Our jobs should not come first, but rather our relationships and our health—physical and mental well-being. It is important that you don't accept all invitations to meetings, banquets, committees, etc. Sometimes you need to take a break and get away from everything. Ephesians 5:15-16 says, "See then that you walk circumspectly, not as fools but as wise, redeeming the time, because the days are evil."

Learn not to worry about calls from people asking you to meet a need that you do not have the resources for. If you do not have it, be sensitive and wise by saying, "Sorry, I don't have that to help you," and don't feel guilty about it. Some believers worry too much over what is not in their power to change. We must learn to not worry over things we cannot handle. Our worry will never fix them for us. Philippians 4:6-7 says:

Be anxious for nothing, but in everything by prayer and supplication, with thanksgiving, let your requests be made known to God; and the peace of God, which surpasses all understanding, will guard your hearts and minds through Christ Jesus.

The peace of God can take root inside of you only when you give to God what you cannot handle and quit worrying.

Also, having an unhealthy competitive mind can cause you pain and unnecessary stress. It is unhealthy when your drive for success is totally geared toward being better than that "other better." That the person you helped in some way yesterday has bought a new car or has moved into a bigger house should not alarm you or cause you to despair. That your colleagues are now flying in a first class cabin while you are still flying economy does not depreciate the progress that you are making in your life. Remember, God's program for that person is different from His program for you.

Do not allow somebody else's achievements to stress you and make you ill. Do not seek or try to be better than others. Just be your best, be productive and contented with what God is doing in you, do not measure your attainment by somebody else's achievement. Always look on the brighter side of life; seldom are things as bad as you think. You may not realize it, but there is something good God is doing in you, and there is something you have that somebody somewhere is wishing they had. When you are going through challenges, try to see things from God's perspective. He says in Romans 8:28, "And we know that all things work together for good to those who love God, to those who are the called according to His purpose." God is always in full control; and no matter what, He is going to work out His plan for you. Scripture calls Him the Author and Finisher of our faith:

> *Therefore we also, since we are surrounded by so great a cloud of witnesses, let us lay aside every weight, and the sin which so easily ensnares us, and let us run with endurance the race that is set before us, looking unto Jesus, the author and finisher of our faith, who for the joy that was set before Him endured the cross, despising the shame, and has sat down at the right hand of the throne of God (Hebrews 12:1-2).*

Another cause of stress is bitterness, life can become bitter for us when we let bitterness in. Do not allow bitterness to infiltrate your heart against anybody. When you have an issue with somebody, you must make room for reconciliation and try to deal with it as soon as possible. Do not allow it to develop into a monster. Matthew 5:23-24 says:

> *Therefore if you bring your gift to the altar, and there remember that your brother has something against you, leave your gift there before the altar, and go your way. First be reconciled to your brother, and then come and offer your gift.*

You can see from these verses that offense can even stand in the way of your worship. No matter how small the problem between you and somebody, it is significant in the spirit realm. If you can't deal with the problem and let go, the altar will not respond to you; it will reject the sacrifice. The altar is what links humanity with Diety, and it is the carrier or conveyer of your worship and spiritual sacrifices. God will accept what is placed on the altar only when the giver is at peace with God or is seeking His peace, when the giver is at peace with himself, and when he is at peace with his brother.

Offense happens, it is part of human nature; it happens even between the best of friends who have good intentions toward each other. The root of offense can come from the devil who is seeking to use it to separate two people so they do not fulfill their destiny together. I have seen people sink into depression as a direct result of being offended and then isolate themselves from people who really care and want to help them. Do whatever you can not to isolate yourself and be lonely—no matter what has come between you and the other person.

Loneliness can lead to depression, and depression is a thief of joy. When you lose joy, life loses its meaning and nothing satisfies you anymore. When nothing motivates or satisfies you anymore, you don't want to fight for anything, and you feel as if you do not have anything to live for—all you want to do is die. This is the point to which the devil has succeeded in bringing millions of people who have committed or attempted to commit suicide. Cherish the life God gave you—don't allow satan to have his way with you.

The Joy of the Lord Is Medicine

The joy of the Lord is medicine to the human soul. Joy is a criterion to finding fulfillment not only in the things we do, but in life itself. You must look for ways to maintain the joy of the Lord inside you. There are two kinds of joy: the worldly type and the joy in the Holy Ghost or the joy of the Lord. Worldly joy is about being happy and is born out of good things happening. This joy is momentary, it cannot sustain you. This is why many people walk away from their once-celebrated marriages, many wealthy people commit suicide despite their luxury houses, yachts, private jets, expensive cars, designer clothes, etc. Many celebrities have resorted to drugs and alcohol despite the fame, sex, and money.

What we all need is the joy that comes from God. The joy of the Lord is spiritual excitement inside you, that wonderful feeling of contentment, satisfaction, assurance of tomorrow—and this joy is not dependent on the reality of your circumstance. The joy of the Lord ignites the fire and energy in you that makes you want to get on with something, even when there are no physical indications that things will go right.

Joy is different from happiness. Happiness is the *feeling* of pleasure or satisfaction that is born out of achievement or good occurrences. The joy that comes from God is not bound to an outside event. It is satisfaction inside, it comes from within, and it is not dependent on your circumstances. This is what the prophet Habakkuk experienced when he wrote:

> *Though the fig tree may not blossom, nor fruit be on the vines; though the labor of the olive may fail, and the fields yield no food; though the flock may be cut off from the fold, and there be no herd in the stalls—yet I will rejoice in the Lord, I will joy in the God of my salvation* (Habakkuk 3:17-18).

Joy is the spiritual excitement that energizes you to keep going despite the odds. This joy comes from the Holy Ghost, it is birthed when the light of destiny is kindled in your spirit, it flames up to empower you against the odds and to propel you forward (see 2 Cor. 4:16-18). Joy is an important factor if you want to overcome the odds in life and reach your desired destiny. If the enemy, satan, can steal your joy, he can get you to be depressed, quit school, quit your job, move out of town, end relationships, or even commit suicide. The joy you have inside—the Lord's joy—is what can keep you going even when life becomes challenging.

JOY IS THE SPIRITUAL EXCITEMENT
THAT ENERGIZES YOU TO KEEP GOING
DESPITE THE ODDS.

Without joy inside you, you will live a sad life. Without joy nothing motivates you, and without any motivation, you are not going to be a fighter. That is why the Bible says in Philippians 4:4, "Rejoice in the Lord always. Again I will say, rejoice!" It was joy that kept Jesus going despite the challenges of the cross. Joy ignited as a result of the expectation of a glorious future and was the strength that pulled Him through from His arrest at the garden to the cross and the tomb.

Fixing our eyes on Jesus, the pioneer and perfecter of faith. For the joy set before him he endured the cross, scorning its shame, and sat down at the right hand of the throne of God. Consider him who endured such opposition from sinners, so that you will not grow weary and lose heart (Hebrews 12:2-3 NIV).

The joy and the expectation of having a great tomorrow enables you to despise today's pain and reach forth to what is before you. We all need the joy of the Lord to go through life, especially because of all the challenges that surround us. We need the gift of joy now more than ever in these end times considering the despair, the hopelessness, the joblessness, the wars, the killings, and all that we face in our world today. We are in desperate times. When we read the newspapers or listen to the television or radio news channels, our hearts will fail us if our eyes are not on Jesus.

In these times when the governments of nations are confused, their experts and advisors do not have answers, the banks have failed, and the stock markets have come crashing down, indeed it is only the Lord who can sustain the people. It is the joy of the Lord that can keep us going and trusting for a better tomorrow, that is our place of safety. If we lose joy, we lose our passion for living, we become aware of our limitations, we lose our grip on the things we were once on top of, nothing seems to be working for us anymore, we become depressed and unproductive in our work—and many become suicidal. When we lose the joy of relationship, we want to separate ourselves from people who care about us.

Always remember, the joy of the Lord is your strength.

Moreover, you need to be confident in the fact that God is in full control, the devil cannot overpower God, the devil is not wiser and cannot outsmart God. God never fails. You mean so much to God that Jesus paid with His blood for you to come into relationship with Him. Because Jesus died to bring you to God, in relationship with Him, He will not be careless with you and will withhold nothing good from you. You need to trust Him with your life, with your welfare, and with your future. Trust that nothing will happen to you without God knowing it. Trust that God will not allow anything to come your way—except for what He knows will work out for your good. Trust that in Him your future and destiny are secured.

Many times we find ourselves in unnecessary hardship and pain because we are doing what God has not called us to do. Be careful not to take on a project you are not sure is God's will for you. Do not chase after things that God is not giving you. Do not allow worldly things to have a hold on you; do not chase them like your happiness depends on them. Stop trusting in your abilities as these will fail you. The Bible says, "For by strength no man shall prevail" (1 Sam. 2:9). It also says in Ecclesiastes 9:11:

> I returned and saw under the sun that—the race is not to the swift, nor the battle to the strong, nor bread to the wise, nor riches to men of understanding, nor favor to men of skill; but time and chance happen to them all.

You must not count on what you can do, but rather on the wisdom of God and on the riches of His grace.

Endnotes

1. http://www.imdb.com/name/nm0005023/bio;   accessed June 28, 2012.

2. http://crossstreetproductions.com/earned-celebrities-rags-to-riches-stories; accessed June 28, 2012.

Chapter Four

THE WAY OF
THE BLESSING

The Way of
the Blessing

Now I say that the heir, as long as he is a child, does not differ at all from a slave, though he is master of all, but is under guardians and stewards until the time appointed by the father (Galatians 4:1-2).

Scriptures make it clear that for the believer everything is possible and everything is available. We are heirs of God; and therefore lord of all the wealth of the kingdom. Our Father God desires to meet all our needs according to His riches in glory (see Phil. 4:19). However, I believe that there may be some things in life that God may not allow us to have until an appointed time. It is not the will of God for us to live like servants but rather like heirs and lords of the kingdom's wealth.

The question is whether or not you are ready to walk in the blessing.

God has a plan to bless you, and He is eager to bless you. He is only waiting for you to accept it. Once you are ready, you will step into your appointed time and the blessing that God has planned for you will be activated. The appointed time is determined by God, but you choose when to get there. The time appointed, I believe, is that time when you have grown from childhood to adulthood and are able to handle the affairs of life as God wants you to. We must come to appreciate the truth that there is something God cannot show when the person cannot handle it, there is something God will not give when the person is not able to contain it. You will not know what to do with some things and you may misuse them if you were to receive them when you are not prepared. As such, they may become destructive to you if God gives them to you.

I have a 15-year-old daughter who is my first child; her name is Dorcas, and I love her very much. I desire for her to have and enjoy every good thing in life that I have power to give to her and even more; but I will not give her everything at this stage of her life. Also, there are things my wife and I have planned for her that she cannot know now because she is still a child, and she is not able to manage that information. For example, I have a bank account with funds for her, but she cannot know what is in the account because she cannot handle that knowledge now. I have a car, but she is not allowed to drive it because that is not only against the law, she may be killed. My youngest child is only 6 years of age. He believes that he is going to be the one to inherit my car when he grows big, and even now he fights with his big sisters over it. Sometime he gets in the driver's seat and claims ownership. However, even if his claims were true, I do not think that he would want it by the time he is grown.

The point I am making is that although my 6-year-old claims ownership of my car, he is not mature enough to handle it. I believe God treats us that way. He will not show us some things of the kingdom or allow us access to some kingdom benefits because we are still children, immature and needing tutors. This is why some prayers of believers are not answered right away; they may have been asking amiss, for lustful and selfish reasons. If God would answer all our prayers and give us everything we desire, He may later be forced to, on account of the blessings, turn against us and fight us, because some of what we desire may become snares to us.

You need to grow to know some things about God, you need to grow to experience and walk in some blessings. I am amused at some believers who have just started their journey with God and yet think that they know everything about God and about kingdom affairs—they know more than everybody else. Paul the apostle in writing to the church put it this way:

And now, brethren, I commend you to God, and to the word of His grace, which is able to build you up, and to give you an inheritance among all those who are sanctified (Acts 20:32).

You must grasp the reality that until you are built up and until you grow to a certain level in your relationship with God, there are certain things that God cannot show you. To walk in your kingdom inheritance you must grow. The Word is your food for growth; all growth comes with knowledge, with knowing your responsibilities and being willing to take them, with willingness to pay the price for things you desire to have in life and not just waiting to be spoon-fed. Growth comes with character, fine-tuning, and discipline. Paul the apostle again puts it this way:

When I was a child, I spoke as a child, I understood as a child, I thought as a child; but when I became a man, I put away childish things (1 Corinthians 13:11).

God will decide when it is your appointed time for the blessing to start to follow you; your appointed time will be when you are ready to walk in the blessing, but it will be up to you to qualify for it or make the appointed time to happen. Now I would like to share with you what I think can bring you to that appointed time where the fullness of the blessings of God in Christ will start to flow in your life.

The Fear of the Lord

You need the fear of the Lord established in your heart. There are certain things that a parent may not share with his son or daughter until the child reaches a certain age in life. That might be a time when the parent feels the child has become mature and can understand the weight of what he or she is being told. At the stage when the parent thinks the child is responsible and will know what to do with the information, the parent may start to show the child the family's secrets, the way their business works, who owes the family any money, and things of that nature. You see, God treats us that way too; and one of the areas He desires for us to grow is in the fear of God. The Bible says:

The secret of the Lord is with those who fear Him, and He will show them His covenant (Psalm 25:14).

The fear of God brings believers to the place where God can start to reveal the deep things of His kingdom to them. The fear of God shows that a believer has regard or respect for God. How we relate to God shows the place where we hold Him in our heart. The value we put on the Word of God is a reflection of the place He holds in our heart. Our commitment to walk in obedience to Him shows our value for Him and our dependency on Him. You cannot go through life disregarding God and expect Him to have respect for you. That is not how the kingdom of God works. You cannot treat God disdainfully and expect Him to highly esteem you. How can God show you favor and bring you to a place of great increase when He has no or little meaning in your life? When you start to walk in the fear of God, then God will bring you close to His heart, then He will start to reveal deep things of the covenant to you.

As recorded in Psalm 25:14, it is not possible for anybody to know the covenant or have covenant with God without having the fear of God. The covenant of God involves God releasing the anointing for wealth on the person He is in covenant with. He says in Deuteronomy 8:18, "And you shall remember the Lord your God, for it is He who gives you power to get wealth, that He may establish His covenant which He swore to your fathers, as it is this day." Wealth comes as a result of a covenant with God, but you are not ready for that covenant relationship without the fear of God having a hold on you. How can God enter into a covenant with you if you are not going to walk in it? It says of Abraham that God shared His secret with him, not only because God saw that Abraham was going to walk in it, but that he would also teach his descendants to do so as well:

And the Lord said, "Shall I hide from Abraham what I am doing, since Abraham shall surely become a great and mighty nation, and all the nations of the earth shall be blessed in him? For I have known him, in order that he may command his children and his household after him, that they keep the way of the Lord, to do righteousness and justice, that the Lord may bring to Abraham what He has spoken to him" (Genesis 18:17-19).

Some believers are wondering why they do not have new revelations or understanding of some of the deeper things of God. They wonder why they are not hearing new things from God or why they cannot hear God anymore. If you are at that level, you need to look into your heart for the answers to these questions. What is the value you place on God's Word? When He showed you what you were to do the last time, did you obey and do as He said? If God starts to lead you in any particular way today, will you listen and do as He says? God will not reveal anything to a person unless that person will do something with it:

> *The secret things belong to the Lord our God, but those things which are revealed belong to us and to our children forever, that we may do all the words of this law* (Deuteronomy 29:29).

Look at these following Scriptures, they show the blessing that will follow the person who fears God and walks in His ways:

> *Blessed is every one who fears the Lord, who walks in His ways. When you eat the labor of your hands, you shall be happy, and it shall be well with you. Your wife shall be like a fruitful vine in the very heart of your house, your children like olive plants all around your table. Behold, thus shall the man be blessed who fears the Lord* (Psalm 128:1-4).

> *He will bless those who fear the Lord, both small and great. May the Lord give you increase more and more, you and your children* (Psalm 115:13-14).

Be Willing and Ready to Pay the Price

You will always have a price to pay to access the next level. There is always something you must do to make something happen. Your willingness to pay the price for the next stage in your life is another level of growth that you must achieve to be able to receive from God. Willingness to pay the price shows that you are ready to follow and go all the way with God. You are willing to do whatever God is saying to do to allow destiny to unfold.

Are you willing to pay that price? Are you willing to do anything God will have you do? Can you go all the way? The Bible says:

> *Thus says the Lord, your Redeemer, the Holy One of Israel; I am the Lord your God who teaches you to profit, who leads you by the way you should go* (Isaiah 48:17).

God has a plan for you: a plan to prosper you and give you a future (see Jer. 29:11). He has a great plan to bring you to that place of prosperity. He wants to lead you to it. He says, "I will teach you to profit and will lead you on the way that you should go." Some of the things that He will have you do might not make any sense to you. He may be asking you to sacrifice something very precious, leave town, resign from your job, walk away from certain people, or He may require you to deal with a particular habit, etc. As a minister God, He may be asking you to come apart (be separated from something that may not be an issue to you), or go on a fasting exercise for a length of time that may appear too long a time for you. Anytime God seeks to do something new in people's lives or promote them to a higher level, He always places a demand on them. He asks them to do something to make it happen. If people are not willing or ready to pay that price, they forfeit the things God has planned for them.

I remember hearing Pastor Enoch Adeboye, the general overseer of the Redeemed Christian Church of God (RCCG), share a testimony of how he was believing God to heal thousands of people and empower barren women to conceive during one of the healing meetings he hosts (Holy Ghost service in Lagos, Nigeria). God told him to give away his favorite car, a four wheel drive; it was then that he realized how much he loved that particular car, but he simply obeyed and did what God said. He gave the car to another fellow minister as a seed. During the Holy Ghost service, God came through, healing many thousands of people, and many barren women were healed and eventually became pregnant (including the cases where doctors had said it was impossible for the women to be pregnant).

Today the Holy Ghost service is the largest single Christian gathering in the world attracting people from all around the globe—seating conservatively between 1.5 and 4 million people at each meeting. I believe that God asked for the sacrifice of Pastor Adeboye's car to assess his obedience to God or his level of submission to God. God wanted to know his heart. He says in Isaiah 1:19, "If you are willing and obedient, you shall eat the good of the land." The only reason why some people cannot pass a certain level in life is because they do not want to pay the price. They are not willing to obey God and do what He is saying. There is always a price to pay for greatness. When God made a promise to bless Abraham, He did not just do it, He assessed him first. Abraham stepped into the blessing because he paid the price. God wanted him to leave his home country and his people—and Abraham did. At one point, He said Abraham should send his son, Ishmael, away together with his slave mother—and he did. After Ishmael left, God tested him further and asked Abraham to sacrifice his only son, Isaac—and he was willing to kill Isaac for God. He did not find God's demand easy, but he was willing to go all the way for God. Therefore, God swore an oath to bless Abraham and to multiply him:

> *Then the Angel of the Lord called to Abraham a second time out of heaven, and said: "By Myself I have sworn, says the Lord, because you have done this thing, and have not withheld your son, your only son—blessing I will bless you, and multiplying I will multiply your descendants as the stars of the heaven and as the sand which is on the seashore; and your descendants shall possess the gate of their enemies. In your seed all the nations of the earth shall be blessed, because you have obeyed My voice"* (Genesis 22:15-18).

GOD CAN GIVE TO YOU ONLY WHAT
HE CAN TRUST YOU TO HANDLE.

Another level of growth you must achieve is that level where your trustworthiness is increased before God. If God cannot trust you with something, He cannot give it to you. The Bible says:

> *He who is faithful in what is least is faithful also in much; and he who is unjust in what is least is unjust also in much. Therefore*

if you have not been faithful in the unrighteous mammon, who
will commit to your trust the true riches? (Luke 16:10-11)

God can give to the believer only what He can trust him or her to handle. He gives us according to our capacity. Believers determine the level of trust God can put on them. The believer's level of obedience to God is what determines the level God can trust him or her. The more you yield to God in submission and obedience, the more He can trust you to take charge of certain things. If God cannot trust you with a thing, He cannot put it in your charge.

Can God trust you to use the resources He desires to give you for the purpose He gives them? Can God trust you with more? Can you handle more? God cannot give you more if He cannot trust you with the little you have now. Your level of faithfulness in handling what you have now shows your trustworthiness. God on His part has been faithful in keeping you; you have survived thus far in life because God has kept you. He has kept you because He is not through with you yet; He desires to do more for you, but only you can make that happen.

God is faithful as a Father and will supply your daily bread. He will help you along the way. He helped you reach the level where you are today (whatever that level is), and He wants to take you further; but the reality is that there is a level He cannot take you to if He cannot trust you with it. Can He trust you with great increase? If God will make you wealthier than what you are right now, will you use it for His glory? We all desire for God to make us financially wealthy, but do you know God's mind in the area of prosperity? God brings prosperity for three reasons: first, it is so God can use it to expand His kingdom here on earth; second, for you to help meet needs in the poor and be a blessing; and third, for your enjoyment. He says in Zechariah 1:17, "Again proclaim, saying, 'Thus says the Lord of hosts: My cities shall again spread out through prosperity; the Lord will again comfort Zion, and will again choose Jerusalem.'"

God does not have a problem with us living well and enjoying life. He wants us to enjoy life; and prosperity comes to serve that purpose, just as the Bible also says in First Timothy 6:17, "Command those who are rich in this present age not to be haughty, nor to trust in uncertain riches but in the living God, who gives us richly all things to enjoy."

God wants you to enjoy what He gives to you, but you must understand the order of things as God has put them. He must always come first, not the possessions that He gives to you. If God should bless you with something today, can He have it back tomorrow? If He places a demand on it, can He have it even when you need it to take care of something that is very important to you? Who will come first when your needs and what God is saying to do with what you have are in conflict?

Some people are where they are today and may never experience more because God cannot trust them with more. It is easy for you to say that God can trust you with more, but how faithful are you with the little that you already have? How can God trust you with more when you will not obey Him in the use of what you have now? If God should lift you higher than what you are now, will it cause you to forget Him? Can God trust you with that breakthrough you are believing for? Will it make you so busy that you will no longer have time for God? Will you still have time to serve in your church when the breakthrough comes?

When more money comes, can God use it if He needs it? When you cannot tithe £100 now, will you tithe £10,000 later? If more money comes, will you use it to help the poor? Can God trust you to help plant churches, support missionaries in the field, and release the widow and the orphan from poverty? As a believer of God, can God trust you with more power? Can you be trusted not to use it for personal profit? You are not ready for more if God cannot trust you with more.

You must appreciate the fact that whatever God gives you will be based on stewardship. You must appreciate the fact that God still owns everything (all the silver and the gold and the cattle on a thousand hills are His, see Ps. 50:10), and that He is giving it to you to keep for Him and to use it for His glory. We must account ourselves as ministers of Christ and stewards of the mysteries of God (see 1 Cor. 4:1). If God cannot have it back when He needs it, He cannot commit it into your care. Some people have made pledges before the Lord and told God that if He does something for them, they will do something for Him in return—God came through for them, but they failed to fulfill their pledges and are now saying God will understand.

If He will not do something new in your life, you should understand too, shouldn't you? The Bible says to do unto others what you want them to do to you (see Matt. 7:12).

God Is Your Source

God is your source; allow Him to take the glory for every increase:

Yours, O Lord, is the greatness, the power and the glory, the victory and the majesty; for all that is in heaven and in earth is Yours; Yours is the kingdom, O Lord, and You are exalted as head over all. Both riches and honor come from You, and You reign over all. In Your hand is power and might; in Your hand it is to make great and to give strength to all (1 Chronicles 29:11-12).

Another level of growth that a believer must attain to qualify for kingdom blessings is that level where he or she starts to recognize God's involvement in every stage of life and returns the glory to God for every good thing that happens to him or her. This is the level of growth where the believer becomes aware of the omnipotence of God and recognizes that God upholds everything together by His power. At this level, the believer is acutely aware that nothing happens when God has not allowed it, that life is a gift from God, and that increase and promotion come from God.

You must come to that consciousness where you accept the undeniable truth that God is in control over the universe and that He can never be overpowered by any power or scheme. You must accept that there is a level in life that you will never be able to rise to until God steps in and helps you. Your background, your race, your hard work, your education, and your human connections are limited in themselves without the help of God. You must accept that there are things you cannot have until God gives them to you. You must accept that you cannot and do not have the power to keep anything that you possess unless God protects and keeps them for you. The Bible says:

Unless the Lord builds the house, its builders labor in vain. Unless the Lord watches over the city, the watchmen stand guard in

> *vain. In vain you rise early and stay up late, toiling for food to eat—for he grants sleep to those he loves* (Psalm 127:1-2 NIV).

Your education or qualification, your career prospects, your hard work and all the sleepless nights will be in vain without the help of God in your life. Without the help of God, it is possible for you to work hard in your education and still graduate without a good grade. Without the help of God, it is possible to graduate with good grades and still struggle with getting a fantastic job. Without the help of God, it is possible for you to secure two employments and work a day shift and a night shift and still struggle to pay your bills or have any savings. Without the help of God, you can have a great business idea, invest into a great venture, and it still comes to ruin. Without the help of God, it is possible to till the ground and plant your good seed and not have a good harvest. It is also possible to marry the most beautiful person, the kind of person you have always dreamt about and without the help of God, still have a bad marriage.

The God factor is what makes a great deal of difference in a person's life. We derive our essence from God; without Him, we can do nothing and can amount to nothing. We all need God to survive. We all need God to accomplish anything significant in life. If we do not recognize these truths, we are still children and not ready for a higher level of kingdom blessings.

Every believer must be conscious of three fundamental things about God that He guards jealously: these things He will never give to another and can even kill a person for them. The first is *His Godhood.* For He says we are not to have any other gods—only Him (see Exod. 20:3-5; Matt. 6:24). God cannot stand you having another god in your life and will not commit anything to you that He can see taking His place in your life and becoming a god to you. God can fight anything or take away anything from you that you allow to be a god to you.

The second thing about God that He protects is *His right of vengeance.* For He says, "Vengeance is Mine, I will repay" (Rom. 12:17-20). You must learn not to take on the fight or pay evil for evil but allow God to be the judge. Believers are called to love their enemies and to pray for those who persecute them. You are being like your Father in Heaven when you behave that way. It is a sign of growth. The Bible also says you are to give water to your enemy when he is thirsty and you are to give him food when he is hungry. You must learn to ignore, forgive, and move on—never take on the battle yourself. Always remember that the battle is the Lord's.

The third thing about Himself that God protects is *His glory*. God accepts the glory for everything that He does. He says, "My glory I will not give to another" (Isa. 42:8). Until you start to see God as your source and the reason behind every good thing that comes your way and start to give Him the glory for it, there are heights to which you cannot rise. You must never forget that there is something that your effort will not give you, hard work will not give you, and qualifications will not give you. There are some things that no human being can do for you.

Only God can bring you into a place of great increase, and He can meet every one of your needs. You must grasp the truth that God can bring you into a place of great increase without any of your effort. Never take God for granted; never forget that it is He who gives power to get wealth. You must see Him in all your increase:

> *Beware that you do not forget the Lord your God by not keeping His commandments, His judgments, and His statutes which I command you today, lest—when you have eaten and are full, and have built beautiful houses and dwell in them; and when your herds and your flocks multiply, and your silver and your gold are multiplied, and all that you have is multiplied; when your heart is lifted up, and you forget the Lord your God who brought you out of the land of Egypt, from the house of bondage; then you say in your heart, "My power and the might of my hand have gained me this wealth." And you shall remember the Lord your God, for it is **He who gives you power to get wealth**, that He may establish His covenant which He swore to your fathers, as it is this day* (Deuteronomy 8:11-14,17-18).

God may not do a thing for a believer if He isn't the one getting the glory for it. God may even pull out from what He has started to do in a person's life if He sees that the person is becoming proud and thinking it is his effort rather than attributing the success to God. For God to continue to do wonders in your life (and He is able to do abundantly and beyond what you can ever imagine or ask for), He must take, and you must give Him, all the glory for everything He is doing in your life.

I would like to show you five ways in which you can give God the glory for your increase.

First, you must learn to testify publicly whenever God blesses you. Do not keep it to yourself like it is your own doing. God loves it when we testify. We are showing Him to people. God enjoys doing more for such people, people who give Him all the glory.

> *I have not hidden Your righteousness within my heart; I have declared Your faithfulness and Your salvation; I have not concealed Your lovingkindness and Your truth from the great assembly. Do not withhold Your tender mercies from me, O Lord; let Your lovingkindness and Your truth continually preserve me* (Psalm 40:10-11).

Second, you need to pay for the vows you make to God if you make vows when you are trusting Him to do something for you. You do not have the right to ask God to do something new and more for you if you still owe Him a vow for what He has already done for you:

> *Offer to God thanksgiving, and pay your vows to the Most High. Call upon Me in the day of trouble; I will deliver you, and you shall glorify Me* (Psalm 50:14-15).

Third, you must pay your tithes. You must see your tithes as not giving to a church or any pastor, but rather giving to God. Men may receive it of you here on earth, but the Bible shows that God sees your giving and He receives it in Heaven:

> *Here mortal men receive tithes, but there he receives them, of whom it is witnessed that he lives* (Hebrews 7:8).

Your tithe is the first tenth of your increase, and you give God the glory whenever you give the tithes because by it you show Him that He comes first in the use of your prosperity. Your giving of tithes is another way you recognize God as your source—and that honors Him. You also show through your tithes that what you have is not a god to you, that it has no control over you and you can freely give of it to God. Through your tithes you demonstrate that you are putting your welfare in God's charge and that you trust Him for tomorrow.

Fourth, for God to take the glory for your increases or your wealth, you are to glorify Him in your use of it. The Bible says in First Corinthians 10:31, "Therefore, whether you eat or drink, or whatever you do, do all to the glory of God." You are to use your increase in such a way that it honors Him. It is important that before you use your wealth you first ask yourself where God is placed with regard to it. Ask yourself, "Will God be glorified if I use this money to buy those shoes, that sports equipment, or whatever thing I am thinking of?" God will not be glorified if you use His increase in your life for something that is ungodly like paying a bribe, for drugs, for sex or pornographic material. God will be glorified if you use your increase to meet needs in your family. Every person must work to provide for his household, and it is ungodly not to do so:

But if anyone does not provide for his own, and especially for those of his household, he hath denied the faith, and is worse than an unbeliever (1 Timothy 5:8).

God will be glorified if you use your wealth and resources to support the poor—giving to the poor is God's passion. Anytime a believer gives to the poor, God turns what that person gives into heavenly treasures:

Command those who are rich in this present age not to be haughty, nor to trust in uncertain riches but in the living God, who gives us richly all things to enjoy. Let them do good, that they be rich in good works, ready to give, willing to share, storing up for themselves a good foundation for the time to come, that they may lay hold on eternal life (1 Timothy 6:17-19).

Believers' heavenly treasures determine their level of glory in Heaven; but not only that, the heavenly treasures also build testimonies for them in Heaven. And when they find themselves in need here on earth and call on God, God remembers their giving, and because of it, He answers them (see Ps. 20:1-4).

The fifth way you can glorify God with your wealth is to make a firm decision that no increase will ever make you proud. God cannot stand pride. The way of pride is destruction, not increase; that was why the apostle Paul admonished Timothy to "Charge them that are rich in this world, that they be *not highminded, nor trust in uncertain riches,* but in the living God, who giveth us richly all things to enjoy" (1 Tim. 6:17 King James Version). God cannot give wealth to you if you cannot really handle greatness. If God makes you more than what you are today, will it cause you to be proud? Will you continue to do the things that you are doing today? Will you keep your friends and treat them like you did before your breakthrough and wealth increased? Are you sure having more wealth will not become your god and your curse?

Never forget that God will not hand anything over to you that He knows will replace Him in your life. He knows your heart, and He may be keeping things from you to help you. And as mentioned previously, if you did have them, He may be the one to turn back and fight you because of them. Humility is a decision; no matter how high you rise in life or what you achieve or become, you must show humility—allow God to be your source, your keeper, your rewarder, and your very present help in times of trouble. You must never think you are more important than other people, and therefore everybody must run around you. You must show humility, show weakness before God, and show that you need Him. We all need God to survive; by ourselves we are not sufficient. God's strength is revealed in us only when we are weak:

> *And He said to me, "My grace is sufficient for you, for My strength is made perfect in weakness." Therefore most gladly I will rather boast in my infirmities, that the power of Christ may rest upon me. Therefore I take pleasure in infirmities, in reproaches, in needs, in persecutions, in distresses, for Christ's sake. For when I am weak, then I am strong (2 Corinthians 12:9-10).*

God always uses the weak not the strong, the ignoble not the noble, the foolish not the wise, earthen and empty vessels not the full, the fulfilled, or the proud. We must humble ourselves and show that we are not sufficient of our own in order for Him to fill us, make grace abound toward us, meet our very need, order our path, strengthen and defend us from all harm. We are only qualified for God's help when we are weak and needing of Him. If we humble ourselves, the Word of God says that God will exalt us (see James 4:10).

Chapter Five

YOUR HIGHWAY
TO INCREASE

Your Highway to Increase

Though your beginning was small, yet your latter end would increase abundantly (Job 8:7).

Everybody likes to experience some level of increase or experience breakthrough, and with that move into a higher level of success. The success may be regarding career, marriage, finances, or spirituality. Nobody really prefers stagnancy or retrogression, we all want to see increase or have a breakthrough in all spheres of our lives—and yes, anybody can have increase. Increase is good and it is of God, but it does not happen to anybody accidentally. People have to *do* something to make increase happen. All the people who have ever accomplished anything significant in life did not just wake up one day and suddenly discover that a big change had happened to them without them doing anything to bring it about. We have to do something to attract God's increase in our lives.

YOU MUST DO SOMETHING TO ATTRACT
GOD'S INCREASE IN YOUR LIFE.

God wants you to enlarge your territory, to break forth on every side and be impactful and influential (see Isa. 54:1-4). God does not intend for you to be a "nobody," irrelevant and insignificant to your generation. You are to be a blessing, and it is your increase that can make you that "somebody" God intends you to be. You need to enlarge, to expand, and to grow beyond what you are now. Know that it is God's intention that you experience great increase as an individual. Being in the same position for too long is not God's way of doing things. God is never happy when we are stagnant. Increase or enlargement is certainly God's own way of doing things. You may not start in a big way, but in God's mind, you are to end in a big way. He says in Job 8:7, "Though your beginning was small, yet your latter end would increase abundantly." However, before any increase can happen to us, we have to first prepare for it and do something to make increase come our way. And remember, it is not humility to seek to be small.

Change Your Grasshopper Way of Thinking

There are two fundamental things you must grasp to develop the right mindset. First, you need to know and walk in the consciousness that God is a God of increase. In other words, that He desires everyone to increase and that He is the one who brings the increase (see 1 Cor. 3:6). Second, you need to accept and believe that it is God's will for you to have and experience increase, great and abundant increase (see Job 8:7). You are not God's exception to the rule; you too are to experience and enjoy increase. You must know that God is never going to be glorified through your failure, your stagnancy, or lack of achievement—and that lifestyle does not make you humble or godly in any way. Only the devil is glorified when we fail or are not seeing increase in the things that we do.

The grasshopper's way of thinking reduces somebody to a lesser place than where he ought to be as God intended. A person with a grasshopper mentality sees himself as less than God sees him and undeserving of what God wants him to see as his portion. A person with a grasshopper complex has an inferiority mentality. That was the mentality the people had who came out of Egypt with Moses. God brought them out of bondage in Egypt to take them into the Promised Land. But they all perished in the wilderness because they failed to see themselves as God saw them.

And they gave the children of Israel a bad report of the land which they had spied out, saying, "The land through which we have gone as spies is a land that devours its inhabitants, and all the people whom we saw in it are men of great stature. There we saw the giants (the descendants of Anak came from the giants); and we were like grasshoppers in our own sight, and so we were in their sight (Numbers 13:32-33).

The grasshopper mindset is definitely not of God; the Bible does not say, "You cannot be better than you are today," that "A certain success height is not for people like you," that "You cannot make it," "You cannot grow bigger than you are today because of where you came from or because of your background," or that "You cannot pass that level because nobody has achieved that before." That is a grasshopper way of thinking. You are not going to be able to rise above what you think of yourself. The Bible says "as he thinks in his heart, so is he" (Prov. 23:7).

To be bigger than what you are today, you have got to start thinking bigger. Do not think small, think big. You have got to start talking big, aiming big, and planning big. There is hardly anything you cannot achieve if you set your heart to it, it's only that you have not tried it. Backing down and failing to go for what God says is yours is not humility. There is a difference between walking in humility and having an inferiority complex. Humility is the ability to genuinely stoop down and reach out and relate to people without feeling like you are more important than they are. An inferiority complex is the feeling of weakness, feeling less than others, and feeling inadequate.

Having the right mindset about increase can open you up to more of what is out there for you. Our mindset is very important; that is where our actions are being processed and our impression of ourselves is birthed. A lot of what we accept or experience in life indicates what is going on in our mind realm. It is practically impossible to live a life that is superior to how we think or reason. Even God deals with us in the light of His thoughts concerning us (see Jer. 29:11). You must have the right mindset to have a positive outlook on life, which includes the ability to relate right and handle challenges. You need to accept that God is happy when there is increase and progress in your life. He desires for you to increase—and you *can* increase. God is excited and finds pleasure in your prosperity. Never let the devil or anybody tell you the contrary:

> *Let them shout for joy and be glad, who favor my* **righteous** **cause;** *and let them say continually, "Let the Lord be magnified, who has pleasure in the prosperity of His servant"* (Psalm 35:27).

When you look at that Scripture in Psalm 35 closely, you will see that God considers the way of prosperity as a "righteous cause," a godly aspiration; and when you choose the path of prosperity, you are favoring a righteous cause. God is also saying in this Scripture that the path of prosperity is something to rejoice and be glad about. You must accept that God wants you to prosper; it is the devil that does not want that for you, not God. Seriously, come to think of it, why would God not want you to prosper? He desires for you to enjoy a healthy life, succeed in the things that you do, have a great and fulfilled marriage, have more than enough so you do not only pay your bills, but have surplus to give away to support the poor and fund the gospel. Isn't that a good thing? I am sure you will agree it is. There is nothing evil about being prosperous, it is your portion in Christ Jesus, and you can walk in it if you can start to see yourself in it.

Increase Your Capacity, Increase Your Take

You determine how much God can bring into your life. The vessels you present to God are what He is going to fill. Can you broaden your vision to see yourself as bigger than what you are at the moment? Remember, your vision defines you. Your vision is the picture of your tomorrow. What you see yourself becoming tomorrow is what you are going to work for—and what you work for today is what you are going to get tomorrow. It is good to have a vision, but what is the size of your vision? When you look to the future, what do you see? The bigger your vision is, the bigger the destiny. Do not labor to be small: think big, dream big, aim big, and plan big! It is not pride to do so.

In addition to this mindset, you need to increase your knowledge. Knowledge increases your capacity and your productivity. You become stale if you do not continue to retrain and redevelop yourself. Education increases your awareness. If you remain as you are, you lose touch with what is out there, and you walk in ignorance of the options and opportunities available to you. If you stop learning today, you will become an ignorant person tomorrow.

Education does not only empower you to gain employment and make more money, it increases your influence and ability to touch lives, and it makes you more efficient and effective. A lot of people are less than they should be because of ignorance; their ignorance keeps them in the dark of what is available for them. Knowledge also helps you to make the right decisions. We are all products of our choices, and the choices we make today determine what we are going to be tomorrow. Some people make important decisions based on not enough knowledge; for instance, marrying somebody you know so little about or getting into business you know nothing about. You are preparing to fail if you don't gain the knowledge you need to make wise decisions. Your level of knowledge about a thing most probably determines your level of achievement.

IF YOU STOP LEARNING TODAY, YOU WILL BECOME
AN IGNORANT PERSON TOMORROW.

One of the rules of excellence and achieving great success in life is to never accept being second best when you can be the best. Never give up trying when you know you can make it, and you will eventually make it. I think I need to clarify what I mean by not accepting to be second best. I do not mean you are not to work under anybody; no, that is not what I mean. You see, in my experience in life, I have seen many people who have gone out of a church to start their own church, people who would have been better off and would have been more productive serving under somebody. Some people are at their best serving under somebody.

What I mean is that you are not to accept anything less than what you believe is God's destiny for you. Breakthrough sometimes does not happen the first time you try for it. Sometimes, you have to keep going for your goal and never give up until it is achieved. Never settle for less just because that is the circumstance you have found yourself in. You must be willing to take risks, make a crazy move, and do the extraordinary. You need to make up your mind to follow God as He leads you. You may not always understand why God is leading you that way, but if you are sure it is God leading you, and you know that it is a road in the right direction, just follow it; it is heading to somewhere good.

God is the God of increase; He makes increase happen to all (see 1 Chron. 29:11-12)—if we allow Him fully into our lives. He is willing to and can increase you beyond what you can ever ask for or imagine. For you to experience great increase, God is going to have to lead you to the place where you will walk in increase. He knows where the increase is and knows what you must do to release it. He says, "Thus says the Lord, your Redeemer, the Holy One of Israel: 'I am the Lord your God, who teaches you to profit, who leads you by the way you should go'" (Isa. 48:17). If you desire increase, you must seek to know what God is saying to do to make it happen and not what you think is the best thing to do or what someone else is saying to do. There is a place you may not get to unless God takes you there. He will have to lead you to take you there. He wants to lead you to the right people, the right place, and to the right investment.

Sometimes what He asks you to do as He leads you might appear stupid or unreasonable, but you must know that your increase is tied to your obedience, to whatever He says—even if it does not make any sense to you. God is a wise God and a great investor. He demonstrated that when He invested Jesus into this world and made us joint heirs with Him. Do not be afraid to follow the leading of God for your life because He has your best interest at heart. He says in Jeremiah 29:11, "For I know the thoughts that I think toward you, says the Lord, thoughts of peace and not of evil, to give you a future and a hope." God will never lead you to do anything that will harm you; with God you will never fail, nothing of God fails.

Take the Risk

Investment is one sure way of increase, take the risk. To achieve greatness, you have got to learn to take risks. Be willing to make moves in obedience to God even if it will make people think you have gone mental. You have got to be willing to try something new as well. God can change your plan, your base, your profession, and the direction you are heading. God is dynamic. Do not be afraid of changes. You must have the mind of investment and entrepreneurship. I mean, learn not to eat up everything that comes in as increase or income. Look out for ways to invest your increase. Never forget to invest by giving to God in tithes and offerings. Invest by ministering to the person of God under whom you feed, invest by ministering to your parents, invest by ministering to the poor, the widow and the orphans, invest to support the enlargement of God's kingdom here on earth. Also invest in property, land, gold, stock, etc.

You can look into starting your own business, as having your own business can empower you more than you can ever be empowered by working under somebody. Believers are not to be afraid of starting and owning a business; there is a covenant on your life that God will bless anything your hands find to do. Many believers like to be employed by others, and there is nothing wrong with that, but there is a level of increase one cannot have when working for someone else.

A good example is the story of Jacob and Laban in Genesis 30:25-32. Jacob started to witness personal increase, not corporate increase, only when he requested to have his own flock. Before then, his anointing brought increase only to Laban. You see, the organization you work for is only going to pay you a salary. They may perhaps increase it annually according to inflation rates (no matter the corporate profit) and maybe give you bonuses from time to time just to encourage you to stay on, to keep giving your best and making money for them. However, even with all these incentives, you are never going to be a corporate owner until you buy shares in the organization. However, a better way toward a higher increase is having your own business and trusting God to make it grow. From the story of Joseph told in Genesis 39:1-6, we know that while Joseph was a servant in Potiphar's house, he only made Potiphar great. While a servant in Potiphar's house, Joseph's anointing could only make his master great. You must become sensitive to opportunities open to you and to when God is giving you the lead to get something of your own started.

I encourage you to not be afraid of stepping out and doing something you feel pressed upon by the Lord to do. Fear is one of the things that hinders many people from stepping out and taking control of their destiny. You must deal with your fears and bring them under control in order to make meaningful progress. Fear is a product of feeling. To walk with God, you cannot follow your feelings, you must follow your heart, His leading. For God to take you to that great height, you have got to overcome fear. You must overcome fear to be able to take some crazy steps in life, steps that if you do not take will cause you to remain mediocre. You must overcome fear for God to take you on a path nobody has trodden before. You must overcome fear to be a pioneer. You must overcome fear to defeat the ordinary and to break away from the mundane and do something extraordinary.

It is upsetting to know how many people are living as though they are mediocre, not because they have no potential in them and not because they have no ambition, but because fear is holding them down. You must overcome fear to reach the moon. You are a pioneer. There is something for which you are ordained; but to achieve it, you must overcome your fears. If you cannot overcome your fears, you cannot reach your highest potential. Fear is of the devil (see 2 Tim. 1:7). The devil uses fear just as God uses faith. He uses it to keep his victims under bondage.

Make Yourself Marketable

There is something you carry in you that the world is looking for. You need to be discovered because someone out there needs your wisdom, your gift, and your service. The Bible informs us that even "the creature waiteth for the manifestation of the sons of God" (Rom. 8:19 King James Version). You must find ways to present yourself to the world as having what they need. People came from all the surrounding towns and cities seeking Jesus, as His fame was spread abroad (see Matt. 4:23-25).

People need to see something in you to make them want to connect with you. When you are not marketable, nobody considers you of any relevance. To market yourself, you need to show that you are worth more than you look, that your race, background, or class is immaterial and that you are different from the others. You need to demonstrate your difference and your worth not only in words but in your work, in your dealings with people, and in your character. I want to show you ways you can achieve these.

First, it is important for you to discover your area of gifting, where you are naturally endowed, the thing you are naturally good at, or what you enjoy doing the most—then stick to it. The Bible says, "A man's gift makes room for him, and brings him before great men" (Prov. 18:16). It is what you are good at that will introduce you to people. Your gift, if developed, will make you productive, relevant to people, and sought after. Nobody is attracted to mediocrity, nobody goes looking for people who have nothing to offer.

I am of the opinion that nobody should be good at one thing only; however, I also subscribe to the view that if one wants to be great, he or she must identify one thing that he or she is very good at, develop more skills, and increase efficiency in the thing. Don't just be everywhere, into everything and engaging whatever comes your way. When you stick with one thing, you will grow in it, you will develop skills and efficiency in it, you will build your name with it, and it will bring you before great people. Michael Jordan is famous because of his skills playing basketball, Whitney Houston was a famous singer, Tiger Woods is a famous golfer, Roger Federer is a famous tennis player, Marilyn Monroe was a famous actress, J.K. Rowling is famous for her writings. All these people exercised themselves in their gifts; they developed their talents, and became very good and accomplished in their fields. You too have a gift, you too can be very good at your gift, which can make you great and can inspire millions.

Second, you must commit to hard work. God does not bless laziness, He only blesses hard work. If you look through history, you will see that all the people who have achieved anything significant were focused, persistent, and hardworking people. Laziness does not attract people to you. A lazy person is a waster. The Bible puts it this way: "A lazy person is as bad as someone who destroys things" (Prov. 18:9 NLT). I know hard work alone does not make people successful; however, it is something that enables a person to rise to a place of success. I once had the rare privilege of enjoying private time with a wise man, Pastor Enoch Adeboye, general overseer of RCCG. He said some things to me during that meeting that were worth a million pounds. One of the things he said was, "As a young man, you must be hardworking because a time will come when you can't work anymore. When you are old and retired, you want to know that you are resting from work." He also said, "When you run and find yourself in the front, you become a front-runner; but you will need to keeping running to stay in the front as there are other people running behind you who are also seeking your place." There is no room for complacency in the scheme of success.

Hard work starts when you see the value in what you have, commit to engaging it like it has worth. Hard work means that your life depends on accomplishing your goal, and it does not matter how little it looks right now, you are going to give it your very best. Hard work starts when you choose to stop complaining about your job or career, no matter the condition, and put your heart into it, and find ways to enjoy it—thanking God that you have it. Hard work involves placing value on your colleagues and those you are connected with through your work. You need to start seeing them as relevant to your destiny and make a decision to work with them irrespective of who they are.

Your opinion of your work and the people connected to it affects your attitude. Your attitude will make you a great and valuable colleague and member of staff—or a waste of space and a burden. Your attitude can get you fired or promoted. When you are able to see your work as something good and as a gift from God and the people you have to deal with as potential destiny makers, you will start to commit time and energy to make everything work. Ecclesiastes 9:10 says, "Whatever your hand finds to do, do it with your might; for there is no work or device or knowledge or wisdom in the grave where you are going."

Hard work requires that you commit your all or give your best to whatever your hand finds to do. When you are committed, you will also commit to doing the extras associated with your work. You will start to see the need to volunteer to do that job that your colleagues will not do, and you will not ask to be paid for it. You will learn to stay at your workplace beyond your contracted hours if need be without asking to be paid for it. You will learn to assist your colleagues do their job when they need help. To add, you are also not going to worry over whether colleagues are taking you for granted or not, you are just going to go ahead and do what you have to do because you know it is the right thing to do.

Hard work means you are going to start to do what you know is right to do without being told to do it. Being self-motivated, self-instructive, always going the extra mile even when you are not going to be paid for it are good qualities that will make room for you anywhere in the world. Consider the following Scriptures:

> *So likewise you, when you have done all those things which you are commanded, say, "We are unprofitable servants. We have done what was our duty to do"* (Luke 17:10).

> *Bondservants, obey in all things your masters according to the flesh, not with eyeservice, as men-pleasers, but in sincerity of heart, fearing God. And whatever you do, do it heartily, as to the Lord and not to men, knowing that from the Lord you will receive the reward of the inheritance; for you serve the Lord Christ* (Colossians 3:22-24).

Third, you have to choose to be a person of integrity to make yourself marketable. Integrity is very crucial in attracting and maintaining important relationships. If your integrity is questionable, people are not going to be able to count on you when it really matters. Without integrity, you are going to isolate yourself from the real blessing. Integrity is about being honest, reliable, and being consistent. Your integrity gives you a good name, and a good name always attracts favor:

> *A good name is to be chosen rather than great riches, loving favor rather than silver and gold* (Proverbs 22:1).

According to the Bible, a good name has an aroma or fragrance that can attract more than the most expensive perfume:

A good reputation is more valuable than costly perfume. And the day you die is better than the day you are born (Ecclesiastes 7:1 NLT).

There are various aspects of integrity that I would like to present for you to ponder:

- People with integrity make themselves accountable to others.

- People with integrity make promises or pledges and keep them even when it hurts to do so.

- People with integrity say only what they mean and mean whatever they say.

- Those with integrity keep secrets.

- People with integrity are loyal to friends and partners.

- People with integrity defend and protect the interests of others.

- Those with integrity do not defraud.

- People with integrity do not keep what does not belong to them.

- People with integrity return money when overpaid.

- Those with integrity pay what they owe.

- People with integrity avoid buying anything on credit if they are not sure they can pay it back on the due date.

- People with integrity pay bills promptly.

- Those with integrity pay their taxes.

- People with integrity will not seek to make money in a dubious manner.

- People with integrity will not falsify documents.

- Those with integrity will not bear false witness, lie about others.

- People with integrity deal honestly with others.

- People with integrity do not gossip, backbite, or slander others.

- Those with integrity are punctual.

- People with integrity will not call off sick when they are not ill.

- People with integrity do not use or take advantage of people.

Fourth, you must esteem faithfulness to attract increase. One of God's criteria for increase is faithfulness. He always requires faithfulness before He commands His increase. If you are not being faithful, you cannot experience God's increase. God does not start with any person at the peak of His purpose for that person; normally, He determines a person's destiny from the start, but starts with the person at the base; from there He leads the person to another level and to the next level until the person arrives at his or her destiny. God will only lead a person to the next level if He finds the person faithful at the current level.

The journey between the base and the place of destiny involves training, pruning, and testing. In God's scheme of things, you will have to prove your worth at every level before you can be moved to the next level. If God can find you faithful at each level, He continues to lift you up the ladder until you arrive.

> *Whoever can be trusted with very little can also be trusted with much, and whoever is dishonest with very little will also be dishonest with much. So if you have not been trustworthy* [faithful] *in handling worldly wealth, who will trust you with true riches? And if you have not been trustworthy* [faithful] *with someone else's property, who will give you property of your own?* (Luke 16:10-12 NIV)

If God can find you trustworthy, faithful, with a cleaning job, He can trust you with a managerial job. If as a pastor He can find you faithful with a congregation of 50 people, He can trust you with a congregation of 100 people. If He can find you faithful with some money, He can trust you with much more money. If He cannot find you faithful at this level, He will not take you to the next level. Faithfulness, trustworthiness, is a key criterion that God looks out for when He seeks to commit something to a person (see 1 Cor. 4:2).

Faithfulness involves knowing what God requires you to do with a thing and doing so accordingly. For example, as a custodian of God's people, you must deal with them in the fear of God, "watching over them—not because you must, but because you are willing, as God wants you to be; not pursuing dishonest gain, but eager to serve; not lording it over those entrusted to you, but being examples to the flock" (1 Pet. 5:2-3 NIV). As a custodian of the gift of insight into the Word of God, you must pass it on to others (see 2 Tim. 2:2). You must teach it with pure motives and not for material gain. As a custodian of kingdom wealth, you must give the tithes, fund the work of the gospel, and give to meet the needs of the poor. If you are employed, serve your boss like it is unto Christ, and seek the profit of the place. Avoid calling off sick unnecessarily. Be punctual to work and do not stay beyond the allotted time when you have a break. Do not work just to earn your pay; seek to bring profit and to promote the interest of your boss. The Bible says, "And if you have not been faithful in what is another man's, who will give you what is your own?" (Luke 16:12).

You will not be promoted if you are not being faithful or trustworthy; you will stay where you are or even get fired. Whenever a need arises to downsize a company, usually the unfaithful and ineffective people are at the top of the list to terminate. Note that when you find yourself stuck in one position for a significant amount of time, making no headway, three things might be responsible for that.

First, it could be that you are being attacked by the enemy. If it is an attack, prayers can clear the way for you. The second reason might be that you are on an assignment that God has not assigned to you. We know that God only gives grace in line with His gift (see Eph. 4:7), so you may actually be taking on a responsibility that you have no capacity for, which will always be difficult. The third reason why increase might not happen could be because God has found you to be unfaithful in some way. God Himself can stand in the way of somebody He finds to be unfaithful. The Bible makes it clear that even what a person has been given can be taken away and given to another (see Luke 19:22-27).

Let us always be aware of what God intends for us and keep ever vigilant to be faithful, trustworthy, and full of integrity.

Chapter Six

BECOMING FRUITFUL IN EVERY GOOD WORK

Becoming Fruitful
in Every Good Work

For this reason we also, since the day we heard it, do not cease to pray for you, and to desire that you may be filled with the knowledge of His will in all wisdom and spiritual understanding; that you may walk worthy of the Lord, fully pleasing Him, being fruitful in every good work and increasing in the knowledge of God (Colossians 1:9-10).

My emphasis in this chapter is about being fruitful in every good work. In this regard, there are four important things that the apostle Paul prayed to have happen to the saints in Colosse, according to the Scripture in Colossians 1. All believers need to desire these four things and pray that they happen to them, too.

The first thing Paul prayed about is the need to be filled with the knowledge of God's will in all wisdom and spiritual understanding. We all need the revelation of God; it strenghtens our relationship with Him and reinvigorates our resolve as we face life challenges. We need to know His will at every stage in our lives, as only in His will we are able to find genuine fulfillment in life. Also, we need to know how spiritual things work; there is order in God's kingdom, and we must walk in that order to occupy our covenant place in Christ Jesus.

The second thing Paul prayed for was the need to walk worthy of the Lord unto all pleasing. A believer must maintain constant fellowship with God and live his or her life totally dedicated to pleasing

God in order to experience the working power of God and to enter into the fullness of God's blessing. Believers forfeit a lot that God has in store for them when they are living lives of disobedience.

The third is the need to be fruitful in every good work. We need to do good work; but not just that, we are to be *fruitful* in our good works. Meaning we are to do good works not just to create a good image for ourselves but so we can make a difference in somebody's life. We must focus on having good and lasting results in the things that we do. As we engage our work every day, our passion must remain: to make a positive and lasting impact in the lives of the men and women we seek to touch with our work.

The fourth thing that the apostle Paul prayed about for the church in Colosse was the need to continue to increase in the knowledge of God. God desires that we grow into having deeper knowledge and intimacy with Him daily, and that happens only as we take time out to study His Word and spend much time in the place of prayer. We become stronger, bolder, and better people as we discover more about God.

Blessed to Be Fruitful

You are blessed to be fruitful. As mentioned earlier, God desires that we are being fruitful in everything. That was what He wanted right from the beginning of the creation of man and woman. He pronounced the blessing on them, for the Bible says:

> *Then God blessed them, and God said to them, "Be fruitful and multiply; fill the earth and subdue it; have dominion over the fish of the sea, over the fowl of the air, and over every living thing that moves on the earth"* (Genesis 1:28).

Being blessed is being empowered to succeed, to increase and multiply. Yes, it is God's desire that we are fruitful in every good work and are multiplying daily (see Col. 1:9-10). If you believe that what you have or are engaged in is a gift from God, then know that God desires that you be fruitful in it. As custodians of everything God has put us in charge of, believers are blessed. Because of the blessing of God on believers, we are empowered to be fruitful in every facet. First, we need to be fruitful in our relationship with God; knowing that we are saved and being part of a church is not enough. We must grow daily in our relationship with God. The power of the gospel must impact our lives, reshaping our worldview, transforming our way of life, and making us better citizens, better neighbors, better spouses, and a light and examples to our generation and the next. As a result of our relationship with God being transformed, we will experience quality and peaceful lives, lives filled with hope and assurance.

We are to be fruitful in our studies. As students, we are not to drop out, fail exams, or study something that will not positively impact our lives. We are to look into our course selections and choose only those courses that will benefit us in the future. After our studies, it should be observed that we have improved our lives as a result of our education. Our time in college or university or taking online classes must never appear as a waste.

Likewise, we need to be fruitful in our marriage and family life. Fruitfulness in your marriage is not just about having children, it is more about having a relationship that is beneficial to you both. Your spouse should be able to say, "Look at what I have become since becoming part of this person, see how I have increased!" A fruitful relationship, by reason of their union, is one in which both are inspired to pursue and fulfill their life dreams and brings increase to each of them. Have a think, is your marriage inspiring and empowering your spouse to become the best he or she can be?

We are empowered to be fruitful in whatever we have invested in. Fruitfulness in your investments means that you are to make profit and not suffer loss. We are to be fruitful in all relationships that we form. Fruitfulness in relationships with people means that anybody you meet must be impacted by what you have to give. It also means you are being a blessing, an inspiration, and a source of joy to the people in your life. The people you meet must remember you for good.

When You Are Fruitful, God Is Glorified

To be a fruitful person means that there must be results, good results, in all your endeavors. Your contribution to people you are connected to must be effective and life changing. Your workplace must see value in you. Your contribution to your workplace must be excellent and incomparable. You must make yourself a valued member of the staff, and when you leave, you should be missed. Fruitfulness brings us to a place of increase; and as we increase in life, we become great and more influential, our fruitfulness glorifies God (see John 15:8). People do not witness any fruit in what they do by chance; it comes as a by-product of good planning, investment, and hard work. We are going to explore the virtues that Peter the apostle put across to us, in his second letter to the church, as catalysts of fruitfulness. He says if they be in you and abound, they will keep you from being barren or unfruitful:

> *But also for this very reason, **giving all diligence**, add to your faith virtue, to virtue knowledge, to knowledge self-control, to self-control perseverance, to perseverance godliness, to godliness brotherly kindness, and to brotherly kindness love. For if these things are yours and abound, **you will be neither barren nor unfruitful in the knowledge of our Lord Jesus Christ** (2 Peter 1:5-8).*

Giving All Diligence—Your Pass to the Palace

You must give yourself to all diligence to succeed in the things that you do. Diligence will not only make you fruitful, it will bring you before kings (see Prov. 22:29). To give yourself to diligence means doing your work with a sense of devotion, engaging it efficiently, thoroughly, and paying attention to detail. You must learn not to be a nonchalant worker, but rather be organized and thorough. When you are nonchalant and disorganized, you leave everything to chance, your work will not make any impact, and you give people the chance to disrespect you. The Scriptures admonish that you are to engage your work with your might:

> *Whatever your hand finds to do, do it with your might; for there is no work, nor device or knowledge or wisdom in the grave where you are going (Ecclesiastes 9:10).*

Wherever you are, whatever you are doing, learn to do your job with all you have, giving your best like it is service to the Lord. Never make money your prime motivation in what you do, always see yourself first as serving the Lord, wherever you are. Serve in your work joyfully, irrespective of the nature of it, whether it is highly paid or not, whether you own it or not; and never forget, always give it your very best:

> *Bondservants, obey in all things your masters according to the flesh, not with eyeservice, as men-pleasers, but in sincerity of heart, fearing God. And whatever you do, do it heartily, as to the Lord and not to men, knowing that from the Lord you will receive the reward of the inheritance; for you serve the Lord Christ* (Colossians 3:22-24).

Add Virtue to Faith

Believers must walk by faith. Faith is paramount in our relationship with God and in touching God's ability to subdue and dominate our environment. However, a problem for many believers is not lacking faith—this refers to the belief in the existence of God or in His power to make anything happen, in this sense we all have faith. The challenge has always been in our willingness to *demonstrate* that faith. Faith has a character. It is not only a "thing of the heart" as many people put it. Faith is an expression of God-like behavior: this is the behavior we must allow to show in our everyday walk. Your faith without any virtue or without works is dead faith.

> *So you see, faith by itself isn't enough. Unless it produces good deeds, it is dead and useless. Now someone may argue, "Some people have faith; others have good deeds." But I say, "How can you show me your faith if you don't have good deeds? I will show you my faith by my good deeds"* (James 2:17-18 NLT).

Believers in God must behave in a certain way no matter the circumstances or the people they are dealing with. Faith must be the believer's motivation, not the people around him or her and certainly not the past. One of the virtues of faith is firmness in our stand. A man who shows faith by deeds is not easily moved by his circumstances or the opposition before him; he maintains the course, believing God for the best outcome. A believer who shows faith by deed never pays evil for evil. A believer who shows faith by deed never withholds anything good from people. He or she shows a positive outlook on life and is forgiving and God-like.

Never forget that your faith requires that you add virtue to it otherwise it is a dead faith. Always remember that the virtue of faith is about putting the corresponding action to your faith into practice. The action of faith also includes starting to talk positively, acting in a positive way, sowing your seed of faith, and giving glory to God for everything even before it has been done.

Add Knowledge to Faith

I have heard the subject of blind faith spoken of by many; however, I do not know what they mean by that—faith does not act in ignorance or blindly. Your faith must be anchored on the Word. The Word does not only help to generate faith in the believer, the believer must limit his or her action strictly to the Word of God. You cannot act in contradiction to the Word of God and yet claim to be walking by faith. You need the knowledge of the Word as a guide. You must confine your actions to the Word. Also, faith does not excuse foolishness in the ways of life. That you are a person of faith does not mean that you are not to acquire and increase in secular knowledge; you need to know about finances, wealth creation, hygiene, health, and keeping fit. You need knowledge in the area of your profession; your faith cannot replace the need for knowledge. You may need to go back to school to pursue knowledge. I want to clarify on this subject that you do not go to school to only increase your prospect of gaining good employment and making more money, you go to school to acquire knowledge, and knowledge increases your efficiency and your influence. It equips you with the tools you need to succeed in your endeavors.

You need to keep acquiring knowledge because knowledge increases your earning and learning capacity. Your performance in life and level of productivity can be determined by your level of knowledge. You become stale if you do not continue to retrain and redevelop yourself. Develop yourself both in spiritual things and in the area of your career, try to understand how things around you work;

do not just walk in the dark. Not developing yourself makes you mediocre. Read books covering different fields, not just your line of discipline. Before you embark on anything significant, try to find out as much as possible about the subject. Do not go into anything major; anything that can impact your entire life if you know so little about it:

> *By knowledge the rooms are filled with all precious and pleasant riches. A wise man is strong, yes, a man of knowledge increases strength; for by wise counsel you will wage your own war, and in a multitude of counselors there is safety* (Proverbs 24:4-6).

Given to Temperance—Power to Stay the Course

Another word for temperance is self-control. Temperance is about having restraint or power to hold back from something when you need to. You must have restraint in life to achieve greatness. There is a time for everything. You need to know when to act and when not to act. Without restraint, you will be a person who wastes resources. Many people have squandered opportunities and misused what could have been an investment fund. For lack of restraint, money that could have been used to turn their lives around and change their story has instead been put into shoes, clothes, cars, and food. Without restraint, we drive people away with anger and harsh words. I have seen successful people drive away or walk away from unrestrained people who would have benefitted greatly from their abilities and talents. Without restraint, we become "yes men" even when we need to say no. We must learn to and have the ability to say no when we need to and not feel guilty about it.

Some girls and boys as young as 13 years of age are now parents and have had to leave school to take care of babies because they did not know how to say no. They were willing to destroy their destiny for momentary pleasure, for lack of restraint—just like Esau who sold his birthright for a bowl of soup (see Gen. 25:28-43). Without restraint, we get ourselves into trouble. People are in prison today for manslaughter—killing somebody they actually loved. They did not mean to; they loved the person, but their anger took over. Now they must forfeit their dreams of becoming a doctor, a lawyer, an astronaut, a pilot, the president, and spend their lives in prison—all for lack of restraint. To win this race, we must be temperate:

> *Now every athlete who goes into training **conducts himself temperately and restricts himself in all things**. They do it to win a wreath that will soon wither, but we [do it to receive a crown of eternal blessedness] that cannot wither* (1 Corinthians 9:25 AMP).

Temperance is the ability to put the body under and bring it to subjection. The need to be temperate is necessary because God did not transform your body at the new birth; your body is still capable of doing the same old things. As such, lack of self-control will always result in undisciplined behavior, which always results in loss, pain, and regrets. The race can be challenging, and we sometimes find life to be very rough, tough, and hard. With this in mind, you should still be aware that there will come a thousand and one reasons why you should quit running; but if you are temperate, you will not be stopped. Nothing will stop you; you are going to have the will and power to navigate through all the hurdles of life until you reach your very destiny.

Given to Patience—the Ability to Wait

Patience is the ability to wait for what you believe for without grumbling. It is the ability to contain the pain associated with it for as long as it takes until it is fulfilled. Patience will enable you to endure delay and tolerate offenses and make room for God to work out His will in your life. The promises of God are "yes and amen." Whatever He says, He will do. He will do it, but you will have to wait for God's time. Every vision God gives is for an appointed time, and when the time comes, it shall speak and not tarry. When you plant your seed, the harvest will always come; however, it will take a period of time before the harvest arrives. If you cannot wait for it, you are going to uproot it before the time and forfeit the harvest. There is always a little while before harvest. If you can be patient, harvest will come.

> *For ye have **need of patience**, that after ye have done the will of God, ye might receive the promise. For yet a little while, and he*

that shall come will, and will not tarry (Hebrews 10:36-37 King James Version).

Not having the ability to tolerate delay and wait for the process of birthing to complete is a problem in many people. People have quit jobs, closed down businesses, and walked out of their marriages because they could not wait; they found God to be too slow for them. The ability to patiently wait for what you want to mature is a sign of strength. The ability to wait for what you believe is God's will for you is an indication of faith. An adage from where I come from says, "A patient man can cook a stone soft and enjoy the broth." Meaning a patient person can make anything happen. You need patience. I say there is harvest coming your way, wait for it!

Godliness—Keeping God in Your Boat

Simply put, godliness is having the fear of God and doing things God's way. Godliness is dealing with the character and the integrity of the believer. We must be people of unquestionable character and high integrity. We must speak and stand by the truth at all times. We must present ourselves to the world as being trustworthy. We must defend the innocent, the poor, the fatherless, and the widow. Our belief in God must not be in words only but in our character. Godliness is very important to the kingdom, because we are called to be the light of the world and the salt of the earth; it is our character and integrity that enables the world to see the light in us. When we are godly, living life as God will have us, He establishes His covenant with us, and He starts to trust us with a higher level of increase, just as the Bible says:

> *He will bless those who fear the Lord, both small and great. May the Lord give you increase more and more, you and your children. May you be blessed by the Lord, who made heaven and earth* (Psalm 115:13-15).

The church of our time has lost its influence. Many of the ministers of the gospel have lost their authority because of their lack of character and integrity. There is little or no difference between the life that many believers live and what we see in the world. We cannot cheat, steal, bribe, and defraud like other people do. We cannot divorce our spouses and remarry the following week like we have no moral or ethical standards at all. We cannot chase money, fame, and status like that is what counts most in our lives. The Bible says, "For what shall it profit a man if he gains the whole world, and loses his own soul?" (Mark 8:36).

To a believer, there is no alternative to living a godly life. When we live the "God life," people will trust us and look up to us for answers; we become the standard in our community, our influence increases, and we become voices for God and His kingdom. We lose our authority when the lives we lead are no different from what we see in the world.

Show Kindness

When we show kindness to others, we set in motion the law of seedtime and harvest. We must be kind to people, especially those in the faith. Kindness is about reaching out to people to be a blessing. It is about helping people when they are in need. It is about being considerate regarding people's feelings. It is about being sympathetic to people when they make mistakes and not being judgmental:

And be kind one to another, tenderhearted, forgiving one another, even as God for Christ forgave you (Ephesians 4:32).

Remember that one good turn deserves another. A little kindness today can open a door of favor for you tomorrow. For the Bible says, "For with what judgment you judge, you will be judged; and with the measure you use, it will be measured back to you" (Matt. 7:2). Help people whenever you have the chance—you may be helping an angel. You never can tell, the man you stand with today and show kindness to may be the person you need to rise to your next level tomorrow. When Rebekah offered to be kind to Eliezer, Abraham's servant, and gave him water, she did not have a clue that it was an opportunity God was giving her to connect to the God of Abraham and Isaac. She did not have a clue it was God who was creating a chance for her to become the wife of Issac and the mother of Jacob and Israel (see Gen. 24:11-51). Because of that one act of kindness, Rebekah became the wife of the richest man in the world of their time and the ancestor of our Lord Jesus.

Every opportunity to be kind to somebody is an opportunity to set in motion the law of seedtime and harvest. I know a brother who had a printing press; he worked with me in one of the churches I pastored. He was also involved with the Full Gospel Businessmen's Fellowship. After one of the meetings, he decided to visit and encourage a person who had attended the fellowship for the first time. The brother had no clue who this man was, he only wanted to be supportive and an encouragement. As they talked during his visit, he realized that the man was a territorial bank manager with several banks under his charge. At that time, the brother's bank was in the process of redesigning and reprinting their money wrappers as well as other materials. The kind brother was awarded the contract to do the job, and as a result made millions from the meeting; it changed his status.

The Bible says, "A man who has friends must himself be friendly" (Prov. 18:24). Be friendly and show kindness to people you meet irrespective of their status today. Be available to people, be accessible to people, and be helpful—you never can tell what your kindness will do for somebody or how your own life can be impacted.

Given to Charity—Become a Lender to God

Charity is about walking in love with people; it goes deeper than knowing in your heart that you love somebody. Charity involves providing forgiveness when you are hurt or offended—people often offend each other in relationships. Charity can help us deal with hurts the God kind of way and maintain important relationships. Charity involves sharing your goodness with other people, especially the poor. Giving to the poor is a kingdom investment; and on account of it, God can hear your cry when you find yourself in need of help. Because of your giving, He can open a great door of blessing for you:

> *He who gives to the poor will not lack, but he who hides his eyes will have many curses* (Proverbs 28:27).

Whoever is kind to the poor lends to the Lord, and he will re-
ward them for what they have done (Proverbs 19:17 NIV).

As believers we must do the work of charity, giving generously of
our worldly goods. We must learn to forgive easily, no matter the harm
done to us. We must always look for avenues and how to give of our
wealth; we must visit the poor and the afflicted, the sick and those in
prison. This is one of the areas Jesus says He is going to ask us to account for (see Matt. 25:33-40).

Chapter Seven

THE LAW OF SEEDTIME AND HARVEST

The Law of
Seedtime and Harvest

While the earth remains, seedtime and harvest, cold and heat, winter and summer, and day and night shall not cease (Genesis 8:22).

The Scripture in Genesis 8 is clear about seedtime and harvest; and concerning these seasons of life, it says they shall not cease. Seedtime and harvest is the principle of sustainability, re-creation, and increase. God put a seed in a thing to preserve the thing, for it to live on, to help it re-create itself, and to increase. Without the seed, there cannot be harvest; and without harvest, time ceases, nothing increases, and death occurs. The seed is so powerful that it can even have a great effect on your generation after you: what you sow today can impact your entire generation and future generations. You sometimes can walk into a blessing not because of what you have done yourself but because of what somebody in your lineage, who has gone ahead of you, has done on your behalf. John 4:38 puts it this way, "I sent you to reap that for which you have not labored; others have labored, and you have entered into their labors." That is how far the seed can go to touching somebody's posterity.

The seed determines the destiny; it is your seed that carries your future and births it. I have seen that God will not leave a person empty of seeds; He will always put a seed in a person's hand. God will always put a seed in your hand, so you can determine the future you want to have. There is a seed in every increase God brings into your life. Every increase from God comes in the double blessing, the seed and the bread, just as the Bible says in Second Corinthians 9:10-11 (King James Version):

*Now he that ministereth seed to the sower **both minister bread for your food, and multiply your seed sown,** and increase the fruits of your righteousness;) being enriched in every thing to all bountifulness, which causeth through us thanksgiving to God.*

There is always the seed and the bread in what God gives, but the challenge is that a lot of folks see only the bread, and so have consumed both the seed and the bread together. You must learn to separate the seed from the bread, never consume them both, and must always release the seed to work for you. Until your seed is planted and it dies, it abides, remains, alone.

Most assuredly I say to you, unless a grain of wheat falls into the ground and dies, it remains alone; but if it dies, it produces much grain (John 12:24).

God gives you bread for stamina, for nourishment, and for health. But your seed is the carrier of the future, with it you create your tomorrow. It is the seed that determines what you are going to step into in the future. Remember, there can never be any harvest without the planting of seed. God puts the seed in everything He gives to you so that when you sow the seed, you can increase your bread and have more to meet the needs of others and also to increase the seed; every harvest comes with more seed than the former. As you keep increasing the seed via your harvest and you keep sowing, you don't remain on the same level but will experience more of His increase in your life until you reach that level of abundance.

It is equally significant that you are aware that the right time to be planting your seed is not when things are not going right with you and when you are in need of a breakthrough. Don't wait to start sowing seed of faith when things are hard for you. What you need when things are hard is harvest. Plant your seed so it will be ripe to harvest when you need it, don't wait until you need the harvest to start planting your seed. Make seed-sowing a lifestyle, and you will find that when things are hard for you, and you are in need of a breakthrough and open doors of increase, then the seed will start to work for you. The Bible says in Ecclesiastes 12:1 (NIV), "Remember your Creator in the days of your youth, before the days of trouble come and the years approach when you will say, 'I find no pleasure in them.'"

MAKE SEED SOWING A LIFESTYLE.

Your seeds will wait for you in the future and work out something for you when you really need it. If you want to come out of the ordinary, out of the mundane, out of poverty or lack, and out of debt, know that apart from all the financial wisdom and planning and the hard work, you have got to be a giver also. Giving is the kingdom way of sowing seed for the harvest. It is through your giving that you connect with the source of life; the God who blesses and makes increase happen (see Luke 6:38). And it is important that you don't keep sowing or giving the same amount of seed, or the size of your harvest will also not change. The harvest will always be proportionate to the seed that was sown. If you desire to increase your harvest, you will have to increase your seed. Don't keep sowing the seed at one level and expect to step into a greater level of harvest.

To plant seed, start giving to meet needs in the lives of people. Galatians 6:9-10 says, "And let us not grow weary [lose heart] while doing good, for in due season we shall reap if we do not grow weary [lose heart]. Therefore, as we have opportunity, let us do good to all, especially to those who are of the household of the faith." You can also give to meet needs in the kingdom; whenever there is a need in your church, sow into it. Do not complain whenever there is a call to give into a kingdom project or to meet specific needs, as what you say can also work against you. If you cannot afford it, keep quiet. However, always look for ways to sow into something when you have the seed. You may also sow your seed into the kingdom not necessarily to meet any specific need in the church but as an act of faith to believe God for the next level. In this instance, you are sowing for a harvest of open doors and opportunities.

Sowing Seeds

You can also sow a seed to connect with an anointing in a man of God's life. If you are sitting under the teaching ministry of a man of God and his ministry is a blessing to you, you can sow into his life to make room for the grace that is upon his life or his ministry to work for you. We can see a good example of this kind of giving in the case of the prophet Elisha and the Shunammite woman in Second Kings 4:8-17. When the woman of Shunem realized that Elisha was a man of God, on that ground, she built a chamber, guest room, for him. As a result, she attracted his favor and the anointing that was on his life; she received the ability to conceive and bore a son. Also, in First Kings 17:8-24, the anointing on Elijah could impact on the life and destiny of the widow in Zarephath only after he had eaten of her substance.

The outcome of your life and your future will be as a result of the seeds you have planted. If a person is truly anointed of God and has a mandate to minister to your need or help release you into your destiny, one sure way you can release that anointing to work for you is by sowing into that person's life. That is how the law of seedtime and harvest works:

> *Let him who is taught in the word share in all good things with him who teaches. Do not be deceived; God is not mocked; for whatever a man sows, that he will also reap* (Galatians 6:6-7).

Note that the seed you plant today may not yield any harvest immediately, but the time will come when the seeds you have planted will yield for you. Never tire in sowing seed; even when you are not seeing any result, keep sowing. The Word of God cannot be broken, what you are sowing is building a memorial for you in Heaven. And one day when you really need Heaven to help you, your seed will raise a voice for you just like it did for Cornelius:

> *About the ninth hour of the day he saw clearly in a vision an angel of God coming in and saying to him, "Cornelius!" And when he observed him, he was afraid, and said, "What is it, lord?" So he said to him, "***Your prayers and your alms have come up for a memorial before God***"(Acts 10:3-4).*

Our prayers and givings are never in vain; the good Lord always calls them to remembrance, especially in a desperate time, the time we need Heaven to hear us and send us help. It says in Psalm 20:1-3, "May the Lord answer you in the day of trouble; may the name of the God of Jacob defend you; may He send you help from the sanctuary, and strengthen you out of Zion; may He remember all your offerings, and accept your burnt sacrifice." You must not undermine the power of your giving and also never ignore giving to the poor when they cry for help. If you do, God will not look in your direction when you are in crisis and you cry for help:

> *Whoever shuts his ears to the cry of the poor will also cry himself and not be heard* (Proverbs 21:13).

> *He who has pity on the poor lends to the Lord, and He will pay back what he has given* (Proverbs 19:17).

You do not always have to pay or work for something before you get it. With the law of seedtime and harvest, it is not everything you need that you must always work or pay for; harvest can bring it into your life. I know some people do not like to give anything away that they have, they do not bother about the next person's need—they are consumed with their own need, their own challenges, and how much they will have left to save after they have taken care of what is needed. Some people do not give because they do not think the next person's need should be of any concern to them; and as far as they are concerned, everybody should earn his or her own keep.

People in this category also find it odd when they are given gifts of cash or when they are presented with an expensive gift item. They reason that there must be a catch to it; and when they take it, they feel obligated to the giver. I have noticed in some cultures, individuals may not freely give an expensive gift to just anybody: to a family member yes, to a charity organization yes, but giving such a gift to a colleague or a neighbor is considered inappropriate. The views of these people are that giving a gift of great worth makes the receiver indebted to the giver. It is important to renew our minds regarding these views. In being Christ-like and Christ-minded, we are to align with the ways of the kingdom. It is the way of the world's kingdom that no one can have and enjoy what he has not paid for with his own money.

Freely Give, Freely Receive

I have tried to reach out to people in the past, and the first thing I heard them say in response to that gesture is, "Are you sure? You really don't have to, you know." We must learn to freely give and freely receive from others when we are being blessed. It is the way of the kingdom of God. It is not everything you need that you have to work for before you can have it, and it is not everything you need to pay for before you can have it. There are some good things that should happen to you not because you have labored for them or paid for them, but because of the seed that you have sown in the past. Expect that on account of your givings, God will make people give to you, too. In addition, because you gave to meet somebody's need, God will cause others to give to meet your need, too (see Luke 6:38). It is a spiritual law that if you are sowing into people's lives, people will sow back into your life as well.

If everything you have was bought with your money, something is not right. If people are not blessing you, if nobody gives you anything, it is likely that it is because you are not sowing into people's lives. If we are truly to be kingdom investors, we must learn to give freely and not to say no to anybody seeking to bless us. And when we are being blessed by somebody, do not ask, "Are you sure?" Also, do not say, "No, you don't have to, I'm fine." Not only are we blocking our blessing behaving that way, we are also standing in the way of people sowing their seeds.

I have never heard good ground cry out saying, "Please do not sow in me, use your seed on that other ground instead." What sort of ground are you? If you are sowing into people's lives, expect people to bless you back, that is the law of harvest. And always remember, by receiving from people, you are also giving them the chance to sow.

Another reason some people cannot give is because their highest priority is in how much they can gather and keep for themselves. People are particularly interested in how much they can accumulate, how much "rainy day money" they can save. They believe that what they have gathered can safeguard their future. However, only God can guarantee our future; our trust must not be in what we have but in His mercies and grace. Jesus stated that a person's life does not consist in the abundance of the things he possesses (see Luke 12:15). Also, some people like to accumulate possessions and do not easily let go of things because they think that how much they have acquired gives them prestige; it makes them feel rich and important. Many times this is just sheer greed. A person is worthless if he measures himself by his material possessions.

The Bible says, "And what do you benefit if you gain the whole world but lose your own soul? Is anything worth more than your soul?" (Matt. 16:26 NLT). Your worth is not measured by what you have. Everything we have is like a vapor; it can grow wings and vanish all in one day. We have seen people lose everything they have worked hard to build, all in one day during the recent economic recession. We are to measure our worth in the light of our relationships, in the light of who God says we are, and the value we add to people's lives. You must strive to touch and impact people with what you have; plant the seed wherever you find good ground for it.

Regard Not the Wind and Clouds

To continue sowing your seed, you must learn not to observe the wind; in other words your giving must not be dictated by your circumstances or challenges surrounding you. You are to sow by faith:

> *He who observes the wind will not sow, and he who regards the clouds will not reap* (Ecclesiastes 11:4).

Yes, giving can sometimes be a painful exercise. To give away something precious to you or when it is all you have, or in terms of money when you do not have much of it and you have a number of things to take care of, giving can be challenging. It can be tough to give away something that is very dear to you, something that you have worked hard to achieve and you think you need it to make something happen for you. It can be challenging to give away your only car if you know you are going to have to start walking to work; however, that is the time to sow, especially when God says to sow. It pays to plant a seed even when it hurts to do so. The Bible says:

> *Those who sow in tears shall reap in joy. He who continually goes forth weeping, bearing seed for sowing, shall doubtless come again with rejoicing, bringing his sheaves with him* (Psalm 126:5-6).

Without the seed there cannot be the harvest. Everything starts with the seed; you have to plant a seed to have a harvest. Plant your seed even when it is not comfortable to do so. The life and the future of a thing is in the seed—your destiny is in the seed. The seed that you sow today will determine what you will become tomorrow. The seed that you sow will determine the people God will bring your way. The seed that you sow determines where your life is headed and what you will attract in life. And because your seed is so significant for you to reach your destiny, God will make sure that He puts seeds in your hand—but it is up to you what you do with them. Don't eat the seed because it is the most convenient thing to do. Sometimes it may hurt to give, but all the same, give, for it is the right thing to do for harvest to come.

God wants you to enjoy abundance; but without harvest, you cannot have abundance. You may end up living in mediocrity—almost there, but never fully broken through if you keep holding back. Never forget, God is faithful and will always give you a seed to sow to bring you into a wealthy place. If you are a giver, your end will be prosperous; there is no doubt about it, for the soul that is liberal will be made fat (see Prov. 11:25). Do not allow the economic recession to affect your giving. If you do, it will determine how you are going to fare financially. Do not sow once and then get tired of giving because you have not seen any result; make giving a lifestyle, develop the joy of it, and continue to sow until the breakthrough comes. The Bible says it is when the cloud is full that it pours out rain (see Eccles. 11:2-6). Do not stop giving halfway before it is your time. Do not stop before your cloud is full. For when your cloud is full, it will be your time, and your rain will fall.

What Seeds Are You Planting?

If the seed is a good seed, and it is planted and watered, it will always spring out and bring forth a good harvest. The seed is good when it is a precious thing to you. The seed is good when it is not your leftover, something that does not count and you can do without. The seed is good when it costs you a lot to let it go. The seed is good when you are giving it in simple obedience to God and not because it is the convenient thing to do. The seed is good when it is an answer to the cry of the poor, when it is meeting somebody's need. The seed is good when it is sacrificial giving. The seed is good when the primary motive is to enlarge the kingdom and to bring glory to Father God.

The seed that you plant needs to be watered for it to yield for you. You water your seed by expecting the harvest. You have to be expectant after you have planted. There is nothing wrong in giving and expecting God to bring harvest as a result. You water your seed by your confession of faith regarding what you have sown for. If you give believing God for a new job, you need to expect it to come and keep confessing that it is your portion until it materializes. You also water your seed by giving thanks as if it is already done. Continue to thank God for what you are looking forward to as if you know it is already done.

YOUR SEED CAN TURN YOUR LIFE AROUND!

It is very important you are aware that just because you gave money as a seed does not mean that your harvest will always be in monetary form. Harvest in the area of the seed of faith does not necessarily come in the same type of what you have sown. You may not necessarily harvest money because you sow money, or receive more shoes because you sowed shoes; it may return to you in the exact type that you gave, but this is not necessarily so.

What counts in the law of seedtime and harvest is what your faith is reaching out for; you get what you are sowing into by faith. So it is okay to sow a seed of faith in money to believe God for something other than money, like sowing a car to believe God for the fruit of the womb, to pass your exams, or to get a new job. The harvest may not be a harvest of many cars. The kingdom operates differently. For instance, I have a good friend who is an evangelist; he travels around the world holding healing and revival meetings. God spoke to him recently and told him to give away his crusade truck to support the ministry of another fellow minister. Though he needed that truck, as it was an essential tool in his ministry, he still obeyed God and gave it away. A few months later, during one of his healing crusades, some people came up to him and donated a private jet in support of his ministry.

The law of harvest that worked for my friend can work for anybody and anywhere. If you give money as a seed of faith, your harvest might come in the area of inspiration. God can inspire you with kingdom ideas for wealth creation, and you will come up with something that nobody has ever thought of before—it can impact your entire life and bring you to a place of power and influence.

Harvest can also be found in the area of open doors. I know a great number of people who have stepped into employment that people thought they couldn't get, through the use of seed of faith. A lady in our church who was working on a short-term contract as a manager in a hospital was advised by her superior, to start looking for another job because her contract was coming to an end and added that the management was not going to renew it as they had no funding for it. This lady gave an offering as a seed of faith during one of our meetings to trust God for a job. The following week, her superior who advised her to start looking for a new job, informed her that they wanted to make her position permanent if she was interested in continuing in that position.

God can open doors of opportunity for you through your seed. He can make ways where no one can envisage one. He can send you helpers of destiny; you can meet one person and the story of your life will change completely as a result. If you are giving to resource the kingdom, God will protect you from the devourer, because He has found you resourceful and faithful. He will keep you in health and bless you with a long life. You can experience debt cancellation by sowing a seed; yes, God can erase your debt, too. You see, you can write off somebody's debt and expect God to make the same happen for you. He says we have the right to ask Him to erase our debt as we erase that of our debtors (see Matt. 6:12).

Your seed is powerful enough to make anything happen for you if only you can believe it. Your seed can make God command His increase in everything you do. Yes, God can anoint your investment and command increase on it because of your giving. God can, on account of your seed, touch anything in your life. Actually, one of the most common things God touches in our lives because of our seed, is our investments. God cannot rain down money from Heaven, but He can touch what you present to Him and command His increase there. A believer must, therefore, be an investor; he or she must look for something to do that can create wealth. God is an investment-oriented Being. He wants us to invest, and He desires to see increase in everything we are investing into. He says in Job, "though you started with little, you will end with much" (Job 8:7 NLT). Actually, God desires that you should not only increase, but that you are also able to leave an inheritance for your children's children:

> *A good man leaves an inheritance to his children's children, but the wealth of the sinner is stored up for the righteous* (Proverbs 13:22).

God does not want us to live from hand to mouth. By that I mean, after we have worked and are paid our salary and after we have paid all the bills, we do not have anything left over. That we are barely surviving is not the plan of God for us. He says His plan for us is to have life in abundance (see John 10:10). To be successful and prosperous in what we do is the will of God. To experience increase is the will of God. To enjoy surplus is the will of God. To be able to meet needs both in our lives and in other people's lives is the will God for us.

However, to walk in God's increase and enjoy abundance, you must be investment-minded. To be investment-minded means you will be on the lookout for ways of making profit and improving your well-being; and whenever there is a chance to sow or invest, you will take advantage of that and invest—except where you know it will not yield you any dividend.

Have an Investment Mindset

To be investment-minded also means that you are not going to squander your time doing anything that will be a time waster. In other words, you will not give your energy to anything that will not bring you any benefit. You are to sow only in the place where you expect a harvest. Investment-minded is not only about sowing, but sowing where you can have returns. You must start sowing and be expecting returns, which also includes when you invest in the kingdom.

Now can I make myself clear here; I am not talking about not giving to people who cannot give back to you—I mean giving and expecting God to bless your giving and give you a harvest. I have heard some people say, I will give to God and not expect anything in return, which is not the attitude God desires us to have. It is a kingdom principle for us to expect the fulfillment of His promises regarding seedtime and harvest whenever we give. If we do not, we are implying that we do not trust His Word. It is good to give to God primarily because we love Him and because we want to obey His instruction regarding giving. However, because God treats our giving as seeds, it is important to give and trust Him for harvest.

The law of seedtime and harvest is built on the principle that whatever you sow, you will reap. You have got to expect harvest when you sow. When you do not expect harvest or do not sow for harvest, three things can happen: First, you will likely not be sensitive to realize when it is a kingdom planting season, when God is saying to plant a seed for harvest. A chance will open for you to sow a seed so God can take you to a higher level, but you will likely miss it.

Second, you will likely be a waster. As you are not bothered about harvest in your giving, you are not going to be bothered about good ground for your seed, and as such, you will be putting your seed where it is not going to yield anything for you. It is not every ground that can yield the harvest that is life changing. God would like to show you where to plant for that breakthrough; but if you are not bothered about harvest, you are not going to connect to it.

Third, you may not walk in kingdom blessing because the Bible says your expectation shall not be cut off (see Prov. 23:18). What you expect is what you will get. When you expect nothing, you get nothing. If you are a sower, you must expect harvest. The Bible also says:

> **Those who sow** with tears **will reap** with songs of joy. Those who
> go out weeping, carrying seed to sow, will return with songs of
> joy, carrying sheaves with them (Psalm 126:5-6 NIV).

Your life of giving must be based on faith in God's Word. I know
you like to give to the glory of God. I know you like to give just to be
a blessing. I know your giving is an expression of love. That is all
noble and the Christian thing to do; however, you need to also accept
God's idea of giving and receiving, and expect that as a result of your
giving God is able to make all grace abound toward you and make
you have even more sufficiently (see 2 Cor. 9:6-8). If you trust Him
for harvest, He will make harvest come; you will return the glory to
Him for it and will increase in every good work.

Separate Your Seed

You must learn to separate your seed and not eat it with the bread.
Remember, every increase that is from God is in the double blessing;
He gives both seed to the sower and bread to the eater. Another important thing about having an investment mind is the ability to start
to see and treat whatever God gives you as seed first and not as bread.
As the God of increase, He puts the seed in everything He gives to us.
Start naming and taking out the seed first in everything He puts in
your hand and do not see and treat everything as bread. When you
see all that is coming to you as only bread, you will only be a con-
sumer not an investor. Look at what the following verses of Scripture
have to say:

> For as the rain comes down, and the snow from heaven, and do
> not return there, but water the earth, and make it bring forth
> and bud, that it may give seed to the sower and bread to the
> eater, so shall My word be that goes forth from My mouth; it
> shall not return to Me void, but it shall accomplish what I
> please, and it shall prosper in the thing for which I sent it (Isaiah
> 55:10-11).

> Now may He who supplies seed to the sower, and bread for food,
> supply and multiply the seed you have sown and increase the
> fruits of your righteousness, while you are enriched in everything

for all liberality, which causes thanksgiving through us to God
(2 Corinthians 9:10-11).

Can you see that in both Scriptures God indicates He first gives seed to sow and then bread for food? With the seed, He increases your seed for the next planting season; as a result, He multiplies the bread even more. The more seeds you plant, the more your seeds and bread multiply. The problem is that we consume the seed with the bread. A lot of us have consumed our seed. We have our great future—in our bellies! What could have been houses, stocks, land, and great investments are now expensive cars, designer shoes, handbags, clothes, luxurious holidays, etc. The seed could be what you used for that shirt and shoes you really didn't need, that restaurant meal that you could have done without, and the vacation you did not need. Think how much you could have saved or invested if you were more prudent with your money. You will have to be investment-minded and disciplined to put aside the seed. It can be painful to put seed aside and not eat it with the bread. But it is good to suffer affliction today in order to have affluence and influence tomorrow. The Bible says:

> *For our light affliction, which is but for a moment, is working for us a far more exceeding and eternal weight of glory* (2 Corinthians 4:17).

Sometimes, you must allow room for a little affliction and a little hardship in your life for the glory of tomorrow. Do not just be concerned about today's comfort—plan for tomorrow. You do not have to have everything you want today. Today's suffering can make room for tomorrow's supplies. Today's investment can make room for tomorrow's enjoyment. What you give up today can lift you up tomorrow. Today is a passageway to tomorrow; use it wisely. Don't sabotage what is in stock for you in the morrow for today's pleasure.

Always be on the lookout for opportunities to sow for the harvest. Before you start to consume what has come in as an increase, always find out first if it can be turned to a seed. Consider whether there is something you can do with it to turn it to double that size. As a kingdom investor, always be on the lookout for ways and for people you can invest in. It is important that you always remember that there is power for wealth; it comes from God. When God releases the power for wealth on a person, everything he or she touches prospers and yields increase.

To attract this power, you need to continue to plant seeds in the ways mentioned throughout this book. You are to give to advance God's kingdom here on earth, give to charities to support good causes, and give to meet needs in people's lives. You make the law of harvest work for you when you reinvest your increase into the kingdom and into people. This lifestyle of giving makes the heaven over you open and release the power behind increase. When what you have cannot meet your immediate need, consider it to be a seed, look for someone whose need it will meet, and be a blessing to that person, that family.

Whatever the case, you are to listen to what God is saying to do with everything He gives to you. And as you do as He says, He will make your harvest come. Harvest comes in many ways, one of which is what I mentioned earlier, that God will cause others to give to you as well. Remember, you are supposed to work hard and pay your debts, but there are also times when harvest comes by God touching and prospering the work of your hand. So you need to look out for something you can call your own and present it to God so He can touch it. If you have the mind of investment, He will want to show you ways of making profit.

God wants to teach you and lead you in the way of profit (see Isa. 48:17). If you start to look for ways you can invest and multiply your resources, He will show you where to invest and not make a loss. God wants you to get to that level where you are not working for money but for pleasure. He wants you to be at that level where money is working for you. There is a level of increase and abundance that you are not going to be able to experience through a salary from employment. A salary can never make anybody very wealthy. It will only make you a pensioner. Do not plan to live on a pension, but rather plan to live on dividends from investments and on the blessing of God and increase from your own business.

You may be thinking that if you had the money, you would like to invest it in some way. But you see, God will always give seed to the sower. The problem is not whether you are going to have the seed or not, it is whether you are going to sow or eat the seed. If you look around closely, you will see that He has put a seed in your hand; it may be a little seed, but that is where to start. Why not release it today? Start a business and trust the Lord with it.

And I declare, there is breakthrough coming your way!

Chapter Eight

TAKE YOUR KINGDOM
FORCEFULLY

Take Your Kingdom Forcefully

And from the days of John the Baptist until now, the kingdom of heaven suffers violence, and the violent take it by force (Matthew 11:12).

The word "kingdom" is not necessarily referring to a geographical location, it is also used to refer to the area within the will and purpose of God. That was what Jesus had in mind when in teaching His disciples how to pray He said to pray this way, "Our Father which art in heaven, hallowed be thy name. *Thy kingdom come, Thy will be done* in earth, as it is in heaven" (Matt. 6:9-10 King James Version). So the kingdom of God is come when it is His will and purpose that has been done in a place.

To "take the kingdom" means to enter into the will and the purpose of God. To "take the kingdom by force" involves fighting for it. Everybody is created to fulfill a purpose—God's purpose. We are not in this world by accident, nobody is. We are in this world because God has a plan to fulfill in us, for us, and through us.

If you have come into relationship with Jesus, then it is vital you know that God did not save you just to bring you into relationship with Him and that is it. Jesus came into your life so that in relationship with Him, He can empower you to fulfill the purpose for which you were created. Now that you are born again and in relationship with God, you are blessed and can succeed in everything you do. You now have a chance to become what God created you to become.

None of us by destiny is ordained to live a life of failure, misery, or to be a pain or burden for our generation. Every one of us can be very successful in life. We all have the capacity to reach our highest goals. We all can make it, no matter our backgrounds, no matter where we find ourselves, and no matter who we have to contend with. It is true that life is full of challenges, but no challenge that God will allow to come our way has the power to destroy our destiny.

Success is a choice; to achieve a great destiny is a matter of choice. Each of us has the power to choose how we want our end to be. If you are choosing to succeed, there are virtues you must have including expectation, determination, and the winner's complex and commitment. I would like to look at these virtues individually to show you how they can change your life.

Your Expectations—Your Tomorrow

Your expectations in life point to what you are going to become and where you will arrive. Expectation is when you are anticipating something to happen. It is good to hope for something. The Bible says, "It is good that one should hope and wait quietly for the salvation of the Lord" (Lam. 3:26).

The opposite of expectation is despondency. When you expect nothing, nothing happens. When you expect to fail, you become an underachiever. Your expectation defines the quality of your life. It defines what you will have in the future. It is good to have expectations, but it is better to have *positive* expectations. Without positive expectations in life, you will live a sad life, you will become depressed, worry over nothing, and you may even become suicidal. Positive expectation is what makes you alive, passionate, and productive.

Faith is about expectations. If you are walking in faith, you have got to expect something to happen. If you are acting on the Word of God spoken into your life, you have got to expect something to happen. If you are sowing seed, you have to expect the harvest. Faith makes a believer do things; through faith he is able to make sacrifices, sow seeds, and can subject himself to uncomfortable situations. However, it is his expectation that creates the factory that manufactures the future or the harvest. It is the believer's expectation that releases the anointing to make something that he or she labored for happen.

Through positive expectation you develop joy for living and are excited about tomorrow. You overcome fear. You are empowered to become a fighter. You are able to endure difficulty, and obstacles do not deter you. You are not going to put your all into something if you are not certain that something good can come out of it. This is why expectation is critical in our journey to the future, it drives you on and compels you to make all the necessary sacrifices required.

Don't have a life that banks on "whatever will be will be." That is a carefree lifestyle; and with that mindset, you are not going to fight for what is yours and will end up as an underachiever. You need to have a purpose for living, set definite goals and develop a passion to become or achieve it—that must be the driving force in your life. Let everything you do—your effort, hard work, and the sacrifices you make—be directed toward achieving that which you believe is there in the future for you. Having expectations is seeing yourself becoming it; it is seeing all your efforts being translated into good success. If you cannot see it happening, you will walk in defeat, subdued by your circumstance, your potentials suppressed, and your confidence overthrown. I assure you there is something better out there for you. Look out for it and go for it.

Determination—the Warrior Inside You

To succeed in life, you must be prepared to fight for what you believe or stand for. It is determination that develops the fighter spirit in a person. Determination is the mind that is set on achieving something no matter the cost or challenges. Determination insists on succeeding in a thing even when it physically looks impossible. Determination is the courage to confront one's challenges and not give up. Determination is the mindset that does not accept no for an answer but is persuaded that something can be done and must be done. This is why determination is one of the qualities required to enter into the realm of success. You must be a determined person to make it in life. Do some research on your own, you will see that every successful person demonstrated this quality of determination.

Determination is birthed out of a conviction that something can be done and must be done. Determination is another character of faith; it is produced through faith. You recognize a person of faith not when things are going according to plan, but when there are challenges and the person still sticks to his or her conviction. You know a person of faith by how he or she responds to difficulty. A person of faith does not give up in difficult times, he or she holds on to conviction; holds on even when it is not comfortable to do so. Faithful people hold on even when there is no physical indication that something will happen.

Just knowing the promise of God for you is not enough to make you walk in it. You will have to fight with the giants in life and overcome those giants so you can walk in God's promise. Having faith does not mean that things are going to go smoothly. Everybody at some point in his or her life will face a giant. A giant is something that stands before you as a threat or obstacle and seeks to make your life miserable. The giant could be a lack of proper education, a trial in the area of finances, a sickness or disability, joblessness, or even racism. The trial could come in the area of marriage, dealing with bad habits, or even opposition in the workplace. We all know that life is full of challenges, and we all have our challenges.

The enemy, satan, will try to stand in your way to fulfilling God's purpose, and he will attack you wherever you are. He will attack you to defy your God, make you think that God is not real, or make you think that if God is real, then He has lost or has no control and no power over what you are going through and can therefore not help you. The devil attacks believers to undermine their faith, or even overthrow it—make you doubt the promises of God and reject Jesus if possible. He will attack you to subject you to bondage—that is, to afflict, oppress, and make your life sad. He will attack you to destroy your purpose—the devil's ultimate plan is not just to frustrate you; he wants to kill God's plan for your life.

You need to show determination to overcome the battle with the enemy and to take hold of God's promises for your life. To show determination means that you will be willing to do anything, to go to any extent as led by God to see the manifestation of what you are trusting God for. This also means that you will not take no for an answer. There is a fighter in you. Never accept no for an answer, know that there is always a way out. You will eventually break through if only you insist and not let go of your belief in God and yourself as God's child.

A Winner's Complex—Your Self-Image

Having a winner's complex prepares you for the battle that everyone faces in life. Your complex says a lot about you and what you believe about yourself. Your complex is the impression that you have of yourself. The impression that you have of yourself influences your behavior, the way you deal with people, your approach to your work, and your appearance, too. And it determines your level of confidence. A lot of people, though highly gifted, think less of themselves, don't see themselves as winners, as having worth—they feel inferior and helpless.

To be a winner, you must have the mind of a winner. A winner's complex is the attitude or mindset that says, "I have something to offer, I have what it takes to succeed in life, I can do what I am required to do to succeed. Whatever happens, I know that everything will be all right, and I know that I am going to make it." Your enemy, satan, does not want you to feel like that about yourself, he wants you to have the grasshopper complex. The grasshopper mindset, discussed previously, is the impression the people of Israel had of themselves when they beheld the challenge that was before them and the enemy they were going to have to contend with before they could enter into the land that God had given them. They felt inferior, like grasshoppers, and helpless in the face of the challenge they faced, irrespective of God's promise to them. Read what they said among themselves:

> ... *"We are not able to go up against the people, for they are stronger than we." And they gave the children of Israel a bad report of the land which they had spied out, saying, "The land*

through which we have gone as spies is a land that devours its inhabitants, and all the people whom we saw in it are men of great stature. There we saw the giants (the descendants of Anak came from the giants); and we were like grasshoppers in our own sight, and so we were in their sight"(Numbers 13:31-33).

You are always going to have to deal with giants on your way to your land of promise, but there is a giant slayer in you. You are a giant slayer, never see yourself as a grasshopper. Nothing that is of worth in life is ever going to come to you on a platter of gold; you've got to give it what it's worth to earn it. People with a grasshopper complex always magnify their problem or the task that is before them beyond what it really is. They concede defeat even before they begin.

Whatever you think is beyond you is what will elude you. There is nothing that God will bring you to that you can't handle. God will never give you a task and not support you with the tools to work with. There is no problem that God will permit to come your way that you will not have a solution for. Don't underestimate the power that is vested in you. Satan does not want you to see your potential, he wants you to live in fear. He wants you to concentrate only on your problems. He wants you to always feel helpless. He wants you to concentrate on your past failures. He knows that by doing this he can make you feel unworthy to receive God's help. He wants you to have anxieties and worries. He wants you to doubt your future, feel like a failure, and give up hope on life.

To be a winner, you need to make up your mind regarding what you want your end to be. Make up your mind to give it all it takes to achieve it. Make up your mind that it will never be over until God says so. You must overcome your worry, your doubt, and your fear. These three emotions are not from God, He will never use them, they are tools of the devil. Anywhere you see them, know that it is the devil seeking to use them to interrupt your way of life and defeat God's plan for you. Fear makes you weak, worry makes you an unbeliever, and doubt makes you undecided.

To be a winner, you need to be positive and must stay focused no matter what happens. Sometimes things will go wrong, not like you anticipated, but still stay focused. The fact that things are not happening as you want them to be right now does not mean they are never going to happen. God will do it for you—wait for it.

WORRY, DOUBT, AND FEAR ARE TOOLS OF THE DEVIL.

You should not meditate on failure, but on winning. You need to think like a winner, talk about your situation like a winner, and always see victory and not the problem. When you think like a winner, you do not leave your destiny to chance, you believe in it and you work for it. When you feel weak because of a failure, don't let the feeling make you retire or turn back; go ahead and start all over again. You must be willing to start again whenever you experience failure. We all experience failure at some point. Every successful man and woman have failed at some point in their lives. The difference between a failure and a successful person is that one of them gives up trying. Successful people try again and again and again. The dumb thing to do when one fails is to give up and retire, but the smart thing to do is learn lessons from it and begin all over again. Be ready to start all over again and not be ashamed of it. Trying again does not make you a failure—quitting does.

> *For a righteous man may fall seven times and rise again, but the wicked shall fall by calamity* (Proverbs 24:16).

You must make up your mind regarding what you want your end in life to be. Make a decision that it will never be over for you until God says so. Time will not permit me to take you through a journey in the Bible to consider men and women who did not take no for an answer, but who, as a result of their conviction, persisted in the midst of the opposition—and God came through for them and gave them victory. However, to mention a few, there is the story of the boy David in First Samuel 17:22-30 and how everybody's opinion about him was unfavorable. But he recognized his potential, he believed in himself, and he went after the giant like he knew he was going to win—and he did. Blind Bartimaeus in Mark 10:46-52 was silenced by everybody, they sought to stop his progress; but he knew what he wanted, refused to let them stop him—and he received his sight. If only you will not give up. If only you will continue to go for it and fight for it like you believe it is yours. It is only a matter of time—you will achieve great victory.

I am inspired of the Holy Spirit to say to someone reading this book, you are about to cross over and go beyond a limitation that is put before you. You are about to experience victory that will be the first of its kind in your lineage. Your story is just about to change. I charge you to hold on and keep pushing through, something is about to break. Amen!

Commitment—the Dependable You

Commitment is attractive, it will endear you to people, will bring you into success. A successful person is the person who is seeing good results and increase in what he or she does. He is steadily making progress toward the goals he has set for himself. He is not stagnant. He is moving forward and is making an impact. A failure is not the person who has failed before. A failure is the individual who is not achieving anything at all and is resigned to it. He is that person who sees himself as low class and feels inferior. He does not recognize opportunities and has no expectations in life. A failure is a person who has put his hands on several ventures and nothing is producing for him, and he makes excuses for them. He has accepted failure as his destiny.

God does not want anybody to be a failure. You can be a very successful person.

One of the fundamental keys to success in life, be it business, career, studies, marriage, or any form of relationship, is commitment. The Scripture says, "For the eyes of the Lord run to and fro throughout the whole earth, to show Himself strong on behalf of those whose heart is loyal to Him. In this you have done foolishly; therefore from now on you shall have wars" (2 Chron. 16:9). God will only reveal Himself in your situation when you are committed to Him. Similarly, anything that you are committed to will always produce results for you. Anything that God gives to you, whatever it is, has the potential to make you wealthy. God never gives anything, connects you with anybody or brings you into a place if it cannot add any value to you. The Bible says in Proverbs 10:22, "The blessing of the Lord makes one rich, and He adds no sorrow with it."

There is nothing that the Lord gives you to do that cannot bring increase to your life. You see, everything God created carries a blessing. Whatever you have now can bring increase to your life. Whatever you are doing now can bring you great increase. The people you have in your life now who are God-sent can contribute to your greatness in life.

Everything and anything that God has put into your hand has the potential to make you great in life. However, nothing that you have or are connected with will release into your life the blessing it carries until you give it your commitment. It is not the place you reside that determines your destiny. As a covenant person, you can make it anywhere you are located. It is not the name or the kind of job you do that determines how high you will rise in life. I have seen professionals of high standing fail in life; and with the same token, I have also seen uneducated people go into small-scale businesses that have risen to be big capital ventures.

The secret of success has nothing to do with your job title or the description of the duties it entails. The secret is in the help of God and your commitment to whatever you are doing. I see commitment as the resolution the individual makes to give himself to something, to stay with the thing no matter what, and give to the thing whatever it places demands on until it yields to his expectation. Therefore, for you to have a successful marriage, for you to qualify with very good grades from college, for you to have a great relationship with your fiancé or fiancée, for you to achieve business breakthrough or rise to your peak in your career, you will have to make a resolution, a commitment, to stay with it no matter what, and be willing to give what it places demands on until it yields for you.

Commitment Involves Faith

There are two things about faith that concern commitment that I would like you to grasp. First, you need to have faith in yourself. I am not talking about self-confidence here. I mean you need to believe that you have the ability of God in your life to succeed in anything that God has given you to do (see Phil. 4:13). It does not matter how things are working out for you now, you have got to have faith that you will come through and be successful at the end. You must never look down on your capabilities, never feel inadequate or inferior, and never wish you were somebody else. You must believe in yourself, believe that you have a destiny, and believe in what God said you can do. Remember, everybody is gifted, and you are gifted, too. You have the potential; you need to rise to your destiny, it is resident inside you, and you have God working in you to do His good pleasure (see Phil. 2:13).

Remember also that it is not what people say you are or you can do or cannot do that is important; it is what you believe about yourself. When they needed to anoint a king from the house of Jesse, they did not think that the boy David could be the one, even his own father left him out of the line-up; he did not think that David qualified (see 1 Sam. 16:10-14). When David showed up on the battle scene and chose to fight Goliath, nobody thought that he qualified for the fight. The Bible records, "Then David said to Saul, 'Let no man's heart fail because of him; your servant will go and fight with this Philistine.' And Saul said to David, 'You are not able to go against this Philistine to fight with him; for you are a youth, and he a man of war from his youth'" (1 Sam. 17:32-33). Don't let people decide for you what you can accomplish or cannot, it should be your call.

The people who do not know the potential they possess are the ones who quit in the face of any opposition or challenge. Do not be a quitter. Believe that you can go through the rigors of life wherever you find yourself. Believe that you have got the wisdom to deal with anyone God brings you into relationship with, no matter how difficult they are. Believe that you can handle the job you have no matter the challenge. Believe that through your union with Jesus you now have what it takes to succeed in life.

I say to you, you will succeed. It is only a matter of time.

Second, you must have faith in what you are doing. Nobody commits to anything he has no faith in. Before you can come to this level, you need to find out exactly what God wants you to do. If you find out what God wants for you, it does not matter what people call it, you have got to believe that it has the potential to make you success-ful in life. If you do not believe that you are in the right relationship, you can easily walk away. If you do not believe that you are in the right job, the right school, the right course, you will never be happy, and a little challenge will make you walk away. You cannot commit yourself to what you have no faith in. If you do not have faith in what you have or where you are, you are going to be ashamed of associating with it. You will not fight for what you are not proud of; and nothing you are not proud of will yield its good for you.

Commitment Involves Consistency

Commitment and consistency are about the heart of loyalty, reliabil-ity, and stability. Consistency is the ability to remain with a thing through thick and thin. Instability is one of the reasons why a lot of people today are not successful. They go for jack pots; they go for quick results. If what they are doing today appears not to be working out for them, or if they discover they are not happy there, they quickly want to change their location, their job, their church—without stopping to con-sider what it has to do with their future.

This is my nineteenth year as a full-time pastor in the Redeemed Christian Church of God (RCCG). Over the years, I have had a few difficulties with some people in the hierarchy. I considered leaving the mission a few times, but God won't let me. I am grateful to God that I stayed. As a result, my wife and I have personally benefitted a great deal through the life and ministry of General Overseer Pastor E.A. Adeboye and his wife, Pastor Folu Adeboye. I have met fantastic people, had many ministry opportunities, and had the privilege of visiting other nations to teach the Word. Today I feel fulfilled; I am doing what God called me to do, and God has blessed and increased my family in a tremendous way. Actually, I wouldn't be where I am today and doing what I am involved in if I had left RCCG.

It really pays to know exactly where God has put you and stick to it irrespective of whatever challenges you encounter. It is possible to be unhappy with something even in the right place because things can sometimes be difficult even in the right place. It does not matter what is happening where you are. If it is the right place, that is where the blessing is; you must stay there. Instability is the product of lack of commitment, and God does not reward instability:

> *But let him ask in faith, with no doubting, or he who doubts is like a wave of the sea driven and tossed by the wind. For let not that man suppose that he will receive anything from the Lord; he is a double-minded man, unstable in all his ways* (James 1:6-8).

If you believe that where you are today, what you are doing today, and the person you are with is God's will for you, then stay there. Do not be moved by what you are seeing around you; with time, it will bring increase to your life. If you believe that what you have is given to you by God, stay with it, and do not allow the circumstances around to affect you. Do not just base your judgment on now, but rather focus on what you can see it becoming in the future (see Gen. 26:1-4,12-14).

Commitment Involves Drive

The Oxford Advanced Learners Dictionary defines *drive* as "the capacity to get some thing done." That push, that passion or determination inside of you to succeed in life or in what you are involved with is what I refer to as drive. Commitment to a thing releases drive. You have got to have the drive for success in order to succeed in life. If you are someone who is satisfied with whatever happens, you are not going to make it big. You have to be uncomfortable with failure, with being average. You have got to detest it to be free from it. You have got to learn to say no to defeat to rise into your destiny. Drive makes you a determined and persistent person, it makes you a fighter.

Remember that the devil will not sleep while you succeed. He will not celebrate your victory. He will resist you every way he can. In all his plans to deflate you, you have got to be tenacious about what you want. Never take no from that devil, never settle on defeat. God says you are more than a conqueror. A good example of drive is what you can see in the woman with the issue of blood in Mark 5:25-34. This woman could not even be stopped by tradition (see Lev. 15:25-26).

Her passion to get healing sent her everywhere, like a wild fire, seeking help; and despite her loss of blood for many years and the weakness of her body, she found strength to push through the crowd. As Jesus passed through the street, she reached and touched Him saying in her heart, "If I may touch but His clothes, I shall be whole." I imagine this woman being pushed down many times by the stampede of people. I can see her crawling through the crowd on her hands and knees trying to reach Jesus. I can imagine all the insults assaulting her, for she was forbidden by their law to mix with the public, she was unclean and smelled; but her desire and drive for healing empowered her to stay the course. Without drive, nothing motivates you.

Necessary Sacrifice

There is always a price to pay to succeed in anything. If you cannot pay the price, then there may be a height you may never rise to in life. Many people want something but do not want it enough to do anything to get it. I believe that every level of success requires a sacrifice proportionate to that level. There is a sacrifice you must pay to get to the level you want to get to in life. Your willingness to pay the price is determined by the level of your commitment to succeed in the thing. The evidence that you are committed to what you are involved with is your willingness to sacrifice to it whatever it needs to survive. The proof that you are committed to a thing is in your willingness to suffer for it. The proof that you are committed to something is in your willingness to go out of your way for it. You cannot say you are committed to something if you cannot make any sacrifice for it.

If you are committed to God, you will find nothing too much to offer to Him in sacrifice. If you are committed to your spouse and your marriage, you will be willing to give whatever it takes to make it work, likewise your career or business. Mike Murdock said, "If you want to have what you have never got, you have to do what you have never done." Myles Munroe said, "The richest place on the earth is not the gold field of Johannesburg in South Africa and neither is it the oil wells in Kuwait, Iraq and so on [but the], richest place on the earth is the graveyard," because there you find buried, men with visions, ideas and great intelligence that would have turned their generation around. There you will find men who died without accomplishing anything. They died without realizing their goals and dreams. Their brilliant ideas could not be turned into substance; they died without fulfilling God's purpose for their lives. They lacked the drive needed for creativity, and they could not pay the price required to transform their ideas into success.

If you do not want to die wretched, if you do not want to end as a failure in life, if you want to be a blessing to your generation, you have to be bold enough to pay whatever price it takes to realize your God-given vision, and take it forcefully.

Chapter Nine

KILLING KILLERS
OF SUCCESS

Killing Killers
of Success

*After the death of Moses the servant of the Lord, it came to pass that the Lord spoke to Joshua the son of Nun, Moses' assistant, saying: "Moses My servant is dead. Now therefore, **arise, go** over this Jordan, you and all this people, to the land which I am giving to them—the children of Israel. No man shall be able to stand before you all the days of your life; as I was with Moses, so I will be with you. I will not leave you nor forsake you. Only **be strong** and **very courageous**, that you may observe to do according to all the law which Moses My servant commanded you; do not turn from it to the right hand or to the left, that you may prosper wherever you go. This Book of the Law shall not depart from your mouth, but you shall **meditate** in it day and night, that you may observe to do according to all that is written in it. For then **you will make your way prosperous, and then you will have good success"** (Joshua 1:1-2,5,7-8).*

I am confident that by now we can agree that God wants us to be successful people and not failures. He wants us to be people given to excellence, not mediocrity. He wants us to be above and not beneath, the head and not the tail. He desires that as we walk with Him and follow the leading of the Holy Spirit, we will be moving forward steadily and fulfilling His very purpose for our lives. Remember, He is not glorified when we are walking in defeat, under oppression, and are failing in our assignment. Failure in the lives of God's people only brings glory to the enemy, satan.

I believe you are also aware that success is not only about monetary prosperity or material acquisitions; success is about knowing what God created you for, ordering your life in that direction, and fulfilling that purpose. Success is also about being in the right place and being happy there. It is about studying the right course and graduating with good grades. It is about being with the right person in a relationship, and being happy, fulfilled and accomplished. It is about having the right job and rising to the peak of your career. Success is also about business breakthroughs and increase. There is no doubt in my mind that success is God's will for every child of God.

I would like to share six things with you that are success killers so you can identify them if they are in your life, and if you find them, kill them. By success killers, I mean those things that can sabotage or get in the way of your chances of being successful. We are going to look at success killers based on God's dealing with Joshua in Joshua 1:1-8. We will look at how God came to Joshua after the death of Moses and challenged him to rise from despair, confront the challenge before him, and fight to fulfill his destiny.

Prior to this encounter, Joshua had known the mind of God, for God had spoken to him before about taking over Moses' duties. Moses had also spoken to Joshua about it, and he knew what the assignment before him involved. Joshua knew what God was calling him to do, but the death and exit of Moses was overwhelming. I believe Joshua was moved by Moses' death such that he was discouraged and did not know when or how to begin. The size of Moses' shoes were an enormous challenge for him to fill, and he probably thought he could not fit into them. Joshua worked as Moses' servant for about 40 years. He saw the glory of God in the life of Moses; he saw Moses' face shining with splendor when he came down from the very presence of God on the mountaintop. He knew Moses talked with God face to face. Through Moses he saw the power of God; he saw the miracle of the fountain of water gushing out from the rock and how by the hand of Moses the Red Sea parted in two for Israel to walk on dry land. Now because of all the miraculous encounters through the life of Moses that Joshua saw as they journeyed through the wilderness and the sea, the mere thought of him taking over and continuing where Moses left off subdued him.

As Joshua looked at the whole people of Israel, he could see how they loved Moses; they missed their great leader. As they mourned Moses, he must have wondered if he could really fill the gap effectively, and whether he could make the difference, achieve what Moses did, or even more. He must have thought, *If Moses, the man who knew God face to face could not take Israel into the Promised Land before he died, then how will I be able to achieve it?* However, as he lay mourning and feeling downcast, God came through and spoke strongly to Joshua saying, "Moses is dead, now arise" (see Josh. 1:2). God told Joshua what he was going to achieve because God had ordained it and God made a commitment to be with him. God also gave Joshua guides and showed him the ways of prosperity. He made it clear that if Joshua did as he was instructed, God would make his way prosperous and he would have good success. From God's instruction, it was clear that Joshua was the one to be responsible for his own success.

From this we understand and can conclude that every one of us is responsible for the outcome of our lives here on earth. You are where you are today because of the choices you made in the past. What you do from now on, how you behave and the things you commit yourself to, will determine where you are going to arrive in the future. God instructed Joshua that he had to be strong, be of good courage, and had to meditate on the book of the law in order for him to succeed. From all that God said to Joshua, I present to you the six killers of success; the things God was trying to deal with in Joshua, things that would have stood in the way of Joshua's success—and will stand in your way unless you take steps to rid them from your life.

1. The Ghost of the Past

One fundamental thing that every person must know is when to draw a closure to some things and move on. One of the things that could have been a success killer and made Joshua have cold feet was the past. He was so engrossed in Moses' era that he failed to look into the future; therefore, when God showed up, the first thing He did was to awaken Joshua to the reality that Moses was dead. Joshua had to arise, look to the future, and move on:

> *After the death of Moses the servant of the Lord, it came to pass that the Lord spoke to Joshua the son of Nun, Moses' assistant, saying: "Moses My servant is dead. Now therefore, arise, go over this Jordan, you and all this people, to the land which I am giving to them—the children of Israel" (Joshua 1:1-2).*

The past has the potential to keep you down, attack your power of initiative, and blur your vision of tomorrow. You have to put the past behind you, as you cannot be dwelling on the past and make any progress. I would like you to consider what may be "old" in your life, something you are engrossed in and could be hindering your progress. It could be a sense of failure, a feeling of betrayal, the hold of bitterness and unforgiveness, or perhaps a negative comment made by somebody about your race, your weight, or your looks. If you are trapped in it, it's got the potential to stand in your way to the next level. You must deal with it, make a fresh start and move forward. Also, your past achievements can be a hindrance too. So in making a fresh start, you may also need to put the achievements of yesterday behind you and set new and higher goals:

> *No, dear brothers and sisters, I have not achieved it, but I focus on this one thing: Forgetting the past and looking forward to what lies ahead, I press on to reach the end of the race and receive the heavenly prize for which God, through Christ Jesus, is calling us (Philippians 3:13-14 NLT).*

If there is anything in your past that you cannot let go of, it can stand in your way to moving forward. You must know what to do with yesterday's achievement and how to deal with yesterday's misfortune or failure. I realize this was discussed previously, but it is worth emphasizing again. We have all experienced failure. Every successful man or woman has failed at some point in his or her life. Experiencing failure does not signify your end of the road; remember, the difference between a failure and a successful person is that one gives up trying. You must be ready to start all over again and not be ashamed. And don't forget, trying again does not make you a failure—quitting does.

2. Refusing to Walk in Obedience to God's Laws

Our refusal to commit to the Word of God and live our lives in obedience to His Word hinders His blessings and is a killer of success. We stand in the way of God and the plans He has for us and hinder the move of the Holy Spirit in our lives when we refuse to obey His Word. That is why God specifically said to Joshua, "This Book of the law shall not depart from your mouth, but you shall meditate in it day and night." When you do according to what the Word of God says, you will make your way prosperous and have good success. Nobody follows the way of the Word and fails. Nobody follows the way of the Word and is defeated. No one walks in obedience to the Word and does not succeed. People fail only when they do not pay attention to the Word of God. The Word of God never fails. The quality of life you enjoy with God can never be above the level of your obedience to the Word. The more you yield to the Word of God, the more you will see Him working in your life, as the Holy Spirit operates only within the framework of the Word.

When you look in the Bible, you see that God confirms His Word. The Word of God precedes the action of God or the act of God. God acts in response to His Word. Before God does something, He will first release the Word. People have to receive the Word of God and act upon it before God does something in their lives. If you do not know the Word of God, you limit yourself. That is why the Word says, "My people are destroyed for lack of knowledge" (Hosea 4:6). You hinder the move of God in your life when you do not dwell on the Word, feed on the Word, and do the Word.

The Bible says when Jesus was leaving, He instructed the disciples to go into the world and make disciples of all nations and baptize them. The Bible then added that they all went and were preaching as He instructed them; but then God also went with them confirming their words with signs following (see Mark 16:19-20). When you act on the Word as He says to do, He will confirm it with signs following.

God confirms His Word only when we act on it; as such, you cannot live in rebellion to the Word of God and also walk in the anointing and power of the Holy Spirit.

YOU HINDER THE MOVE OF GOD IN YOUR LIFE
WHEN YOU DO NOT DWELL ON THE WORD,
FEED ON THE WORD, AND DO THE WORD.

In Acts 20:32 (NIV), Paul writes, "Now I commit you to God and to the word of his grace, which can build you up and give you an inheritance among all those who are sanctified." The Word of God is able to build you up, and can give you your inheritance; all that God planned for you. If you believe God, then you need to believe in His Word. If you respect God, then you need to take the Word of God seriously and operate in it. Every now and then God directs your life and your affairs through His Word. The Word of God will speak to you in the area of your relationships with others, the Word of God will speak to you in the area of your career, the Word of God will speak to you in the area of your finances, the Word of God will speak to you in the area of your relationship with God, the Word of God will speak to you in every aspect of your life. The Word of God is a guide for you, and every now and then God will speak His Word to you to direct you. He will speak to you as you open your Bible and read, He will speak to you through visions and dreams, through the prophetic office, through the teaching ministry. He speaks to you so that you can have direction in life.

*Thus says the Lord, your Redeemer, the Holy One of Israel: "I am the Lord your God, who **teaches you to profit**, who **leads you by the way you should go"** (Isaiah 48:17).*

You cannot ignore those words in Isaiah 48 and rise to the place of destiny. Everything said by God in His Word, when acted on, brings profit. Sometimes we think the Word of God is grievous, we think the Word of God is hard, and we question why He is making us act that way. But you have to know that God cares so much about you, and He will never lead you to a place or do anything that would harm you.

God has thoughts of good and not evil toward you. What God says to do may not make sense to you, but it will bring profit if you do not ignore it. If you want to kill failure, you need to first kill disobedience to the Word of God.

Many believers operate on the level of mediocrity when God calls us to excellence and good success. Many have not fully maximized the blessing in the kingdom, they are on the periphery, on the edge because their obedience is not complete. There is so much God wants to do for us, for the Bible says He is able to do exceeding abundantly even more than we could ask or think (see Eph. 3:20). When we are obedient, He will take us to higher levels of victory. I challenge you to look into the area of obedience to God. Are you in obedience to God in your relationships? Are you obedient to God with your work? Are you obedient to God with your finances? When your obedience is complete, He releases the fullness of the blessing of the kingdom.

3. Fear

Another killer of success is fear. Joshua needed to show himself strong and courageous for him to effectively occupy his new position and lead Israel. He had to engage in warfare with the enemy to bring the people into the land God had promised. However, to be able to achieve that, he had to overcome his fears. Fear was one of the things God was challenging in Joshua; He promised He was going to be with Joshua as He was with Moses. God promised to be with Joshua wherever he went because He wanted Joshua to become aware and conscious of God's presence with him wherever he was. The consciousness of the presence of God in any person drives out fear. That was what the psalmist understood when he said, "Even though I walk through the darkest valley, I will fear no evil, for you are with me" (Ps. 23:4 NIV).

Fear will stand in your way to destiny. The believer must kill fear; fear of anything and everything. Fear of the enemy, fear of failure, fear of the future, fear of death, fear of becoming disabled, fear of getting cancer, fear of whatever is out there that you can't place your finger on must die and lose all hold on you. Fear is a spirit, and God has not given us the spirit of fear but of power, love, and sound mind. You need to kill every fear so it does not have power over you. Anything that has power over you can influence your actions. Your actions will always determine what you are going to get or where you will arrive in life.

Fear has kept many people from where God wants them to be. There are many people who will not quit their jobs to do something different even though they know in their hearts that they ought to be doing something different. This is because they fear the unknown; they want to stay in their comfort zone. Many people cannot start a business, even though they feel God stirring them to launch out; they are afraid it will fail.

Some people are comfortable keeping some funds in their savings accounts only to get a few pennies as interest at the end of the year. They are comfortable leaving it there because they are afraid that if they put it into a business, they will lose it. Likewise, I have met young people who did not want to start relationships because they had been jilted in the past; someone took advantage of them, so they think that everyone is bad, they are fearful of getting hurt again. If you cannot kill fear, it hinders your progress.

If you look through history, you will see that people who have broken through and achieved something remarkable were risk takers. They broke through uncommon grounds and achieved exploits because they were daring. You have got to be able to take the risk, venture into the unknown, and do something new. You need to allow God to inspire you through your ideas so you can start something that has never been done before. Don't be afraid to venture into new territory; you have no way of knowing if something will work or not work until you try it. Until you try something, you will never know if it will succeed or fail. I know that if God is speaking to you to do something, it will profit, for He says in His Word, "I will teach you to profit, teach you the way to go." God will never lead you to a place where you will incur losses. However, for you to progress, you have to kill fear and obey God as He instructs you.

4. An Inferiority Complex

Having an inferiority complex is the feeling of being inadequate, the feeling of weakness, lowliness, or being of a low standard, and it is a killer of success. You can call it the "not able, not useful, not important, not relevant, not qualified syndrome." Inferiority is a bad disease because what you think about yourself determines what you can do: it determines what climate you are going to create around you, it determines the kind of people you are going to attract, and the standard that you are going to set for yourself. Scripture says that as a person thinks in his or her heart, so that person shall be (see Prov. 33:7).

What you think about yourself and the value you place on yourself counts in life. You have to believe that you are special, that you are gifted, that you are relevant, that you are blessed, and that you are an achiever. There is nothing wrong with you; don't let anybody put that tag on you. You are born a genius and you can handle anything that comes your way. Believe that you have a big God by your side, the God who is able and willing to carry you through anything. He will help you through every moment in life. You have to also believe that because you have a big God, there is nothing too big for you to achieve, and there is no height too high for you to rise to.

The Bible says you can do all things through Christ who strengthens you (see Phil. 4:13). Do not put yourself at the mercy of anybody; you are worth more than that. Your life does not depend on anyone else; do not present yourself like a beggar; you have got God, He is on your side and He will bring to completion every good work He has started in you. There is a difference between humility and timidity. Humility does not mean that you make yourself look like a worthless person. People who feel inferior are people who do not have confidence in themselves; they do not have confidence in their ability. They think they are substandard and they do not deserve any good thing. You have got to kill that mentality; you are not inferior to anyone, you are highly blessed. Your color or race is immaterial, your family line is immaterial, your background is immaterial, and your qualification is immaterial in the sight of God. You are important just as you are. And with God you have a great destiny.

Everyone born of God is blessed. In Christ Jesus nobody is a waste of space; nobody is useless. Everyone is blessed. You are blessed. Never allow anybody to intimidate you or make you look down on yourself. Do not feel less, do not feel inferior, be confident in yourself, and be confident in your God. There is a difference between being shy and having an inferiority complex. Some people hide under the cover of being shy to excuse their lack of guts, assertiveness. A shy person is someone lacking in confidence, especially in public, he is socially withdrawn or reserved.

Inferiority is dealing with someone not knowing his worth, what potentials he possesses, and the level God has lifted him to. In the face of other people's accomplishments, and in the face of challenges, he shells into himself, bows down, feels inadequate. But the Bible says, "I can do all things through Christ who strengthens me" (Phil. 4:13).

You can handle anything, you can do anything, and you can rise to any level because you have Jesus. The Bible says, "He who is in you is greater than he who is in the world" (1 John 4:4). I know it's possible that you have failed before, you have made this blunder or that blunder before, but it has not changed the way God sees you and who you really are. You have what it takes to overcome any challenge of life. You can go through any storm and arrive at the other side victorious. You have the capacity because the Greater One lives inside you. Do not put yourself at the mercy of anybody. Do not make anybody think that without him in your life you can never make it, without him in your life you can never rise or become who God says.

Your life is in Christ; in Him you have your life, "in Him we live and move and have our being" (Acts 17:28). Do not put yourself at the mercy of any person. I am not saying to be arrogant, but be confident. Know that you have a great God, that you are a great person, that you can become everything He has said about you, that you can break through all the odds, that you can reach your goal because God is on your side.

5. The Yoke of Excuse Syndrome

Another killer of success is to make excuses. People under this condition always have reasons why certain things cannot be done, why things cannot be achieved and should not be done. They always admit defeat even before they begin, or they excuse their failure with one reason or the other. These people are failure-oriented people; their mindset is more inclined to failure than success. They envisage failure even where the possibility of achieving success is huge. They come up with excuses like, "I'm not good enough." "I'm too young" or "I'm too old." "I don't know people there who can help me." "I'm not well-educated." "I have this disease or this disability." "People might think that I am..." "What if..." "But my color is..." "But we don't have enough resources." "Many people have tried before and failed." "It is going to be very difficult if not impossible to..." To be a success, you have to believe in yourself, see your potential, and be able to recognize opportunities and know that there is always a way out.

You must learn to see solutions, answers, success, victory, and possibilities where other people do not see them. Even if you actually do fail, you have to continue to believe that what you have received inspiration to do will eventually work. It is said that Thomas Edison, the man who invented the electric light bulb, tried and failed hundreds of times before he perfected his invention. That you failed in something once or twice does not mean that it's never going to work. It was Winston Churchill, former Prime Minister of Great Britain, who said, "Success is going from failure to failure without loss of enthusiasm."[1] Don't quit even before you get started.

If you are the kind of person who always makes excuses, always finds a reason why something should not be done, and you are always looking for reasons why you think something will fail, you have got to deal with that trait today—start to see your world and engage life differently. You have to see your end as God sees it. Inside of you lies so much potential that you do not even realize. There is nothing that the Lord will allow to come your way that you cannot handle. There is no idea that will rise in your brain that you cannot handle. If you can think or imagine it, you can do it.

Do you know why God destroyed the people who lived during the time of Noah? It was not only because of their wicked ways, but because of their imaginations, too. God looked at them and saw that the imagination of men and women was continually focused on evil (see Gen. 6:5-6). Whatever a person can imagine, he or she has the potential to do. No idea will arise in your spirit that you cannot handle.

You are what you imagine. Doors that you think are bigger than what you can handle will not open for you. Opportunities that you think you do not deserve will not come your way. God orders your steps only in the direction of what you believe. God will not throw on you what you will not value. God will not throw on you what you have no capacity for. God will not give you something that He will not give you grace to handle. It was Jesus who said do not "cast your pearls before swine" (Matt. 7:6). God will not give you what you cannot do.

Whatever you have to confront today is something you can handle; do not come up with excuses. Excuses make you stay back, procrastinate; they make you weak; they kill your passion and kill your vision. They attack your ability. They have held you down for too long. They have kept you where you are, for you keep saying, "If only I had money," "If only I knew somebody," "If only I was younger." Kill them—kill the excuses. Start to do what is right today. The past is behind you; the future is before you, and it can be better and brighter than you think. *You can do it.*

6. Lack of Self-Control

People who lack self-control are people who do not have will power or principles in their lives; to them, anything goes. They do not have a sense of order. I am not by any means talking about being rigid here. God is dynamic, so we should be dynamic as well. But we must have a sense of order and must have principles by which we operate. Lack of self-control has ruined a lot of homes, ministries, careers, and businesses. You must learn to say no when you need to say it and never feel guilty about it. People who do not know how to stand their ground and say no when they need to, have made a mess of their destiny. You know a man does not have self-control when he easily yields to pressure and does something that he knows is not right for him to do, something that is against his conviction. He does not have restraint over what he buys when shopping. He does not have control over what he says and cannot maintain confidentiality (see James 3:2). He struggles with bad habits such as gluttony (Prov. 23:1), bad sleeping habits (see Prov. 20:13), uncontrolled anger (see Prov. 14:17), etc.

God said to Joshua, "Only be strong and very courageous, that you may observe to do according to all the law which Moses My servant commanded you; *do not turn from it to the right hand or to the left, that you may prosper wherever you go*" (Josh. 1:7). You may want to underline the following part in your Bible: "do not turn from it to the right hand or to the left, that you may prosper wherever you go." If you want to prosper and succeed, you have got to be disciplined. You have got to apply self-control, and you have got to be somebody who is not to the right today and to the left tomorrow. A double-minded person shall not receive anything from God (see James 1:6-8). God cannot trust people who are not applying self-control or are not disciplined. This means you must make a firm decision to be focused and disciplined.

One of the signs of discipline is commitment. You put your hand to the plow and you do not look back (see Luke 9:62). Sometimes the things that God gives you to handle will attract persecution and they will sometimes attract attacks from the devil. Sometimes on the journey things can become hard and rough. The journey to where you believe God is leading you may become stormy and bumpy and there will be several reasons why you should change course, thinking it is not working, so you may want to try something different instead.

That things are starting to look tough does not necessarily mean you are on the wrong path. Learn to apply restraint and not give in to flip-flopping, changing your mind too easily. When it is about relationships, never say, "I thought it was Deborah, but the way she is behaving these days, I really don't know. I think God is speaking to me now about Lucy." Things will always come up on your way to destiny, things that will give you plenty of reasons why you should switch ground or turn around. In most cases, these things happen to test your level of commitment to the cause and your level of discipline. When you stay focused, you show that you understand that there is something in it for you.

Everything that God gives to you has the ability to transform your life and to make you great. The Bible says that the gift of God makes a person rich (see Prov. 10:22). Everything that God brings into your life can impact your life in ways you never thought possible and make you great. Yes, every gift of God can make you great. Everything that God puts into your hand can transform your life. However, it will never bring forth all that it contains in just one day. It is part of a process that takes time. As such, it is your discipline and self-control that will make you stay with the thing, make you stay the course and keep your hand to the plow and not look back irrespective of your circumstances. However, if today you are here and tomorrow you are there, you kill destiny. God says not to turn to the left nor to the right (see Josh. 1:7).

You may know the Bible story of how Jacob, when he was old and about to die, summoned his sons and blessed them and showed each one of them what his future would be. He based the words he pronounced into their lives on their character or behavior. To Reuben his firstborn, he said, "Reuben, you are my firstborn, my might and the beginning of my strength, the excellency of dignity and the excellency of power. Unstable as water, you shall not excel..." (Gen. 49:3-4). Reuben was born endowed with favor, dignity, and everything that can make a person successful and admirable, but he was given to instability. He was not a disciplined, firm, or reliable person, so his father said he was not going to excel. To excel means to distinguish yourself from the ordinary, to surpass human expectations, overcome all odds, and achieve the very best. No one can excel in life being "unstable as water."

Instability never attracts the blessing of God; it is a killer of success, and you have to kill any instability in your life. A person who is undisciplined is unstable. A person who is unstable is not committed to anything. A person who is not committed to anything responds unwisely to pressure; how a person responds to pressure tells you his or her level of commitment and stability. A person who is unstable is never sure of what he or she really wants in life and is always changing—his or her mind, jobs, moving from one church to another, from one relationship to another, from one thing to another, always jumping up and down and never landing on any target.

Success does not happen by accident. Success is a product of commitment, stability, and discipline. Success happens over a period of time; it is discipline that keeps you on track through the seasons, and you get there over time. Remember that whatever you are involved with will not yield you the ultimate result in one day, it takes time. If you give it all it requires, not because of what you see now but because of what you believe about it, when it is time, it will ripen and become fruitful.

Commitment and stability come out of conviction that what you have is a good thing and that your destiny is tied to it. Out of that conviction you do not get swayed; you do not get moved by what you are hearing and seeing. I see young people who start relationships and when it is not going as beautifully as they expect, because of a few challenges, they say it is not working, that maybe it is no longer the will of God, and they seek to separate. I think they have not understood commitment and stability. The fact that they are having a tough time in the relationship does not change the fact that the relationship itself might be God's will.

Your conviction in all areas of your life is what will keep you through and through. Commitment will make you stable and enable you to deal with problems and pay the price or do whatever it takes to get it working. If you find that you are operating at a level of mediocrity or that you are always starting again, as if going in a circle, know that it is a problem and address it. God did not plan for you to keep stopping halfway and always starting on a new thing without first bringing the former to a conclusive and successful end. The key is to know when God is telling you to move on or when it is the devil trying to distract you and tear down something that God has put in place.

The devil may not know the future, but he recognizes the presence of God, and he recognizes the anointing. When it is your season for a breakthrough, God releases the anointing around your life. The devil recognizes the anointing. He may not know what God is trying to work out in your life, he may not understand what God is going to do, but he can sense that something good is about to happen to you because he sees the anointing. When satan sees the way angels are positioned around you, and as he sees the glory cloud around you, he thinks that God is about to work something out for you. When the devil senses that, he will attack you to disrupt your focus. When the attack is intensified, it is an indication that satan senses the breakthrough is about to happen.

What most Christians do when they are under attack and are being bombarded all around is walk away and start again. God in His faithfulness will reposition them, but then when they are on the verge of another season of breakthrough, they walk away again. They create a circle of pain because of their instability; they lack self-control. They are as unstable as the waters, so they do not prosper.

To succeed in life, you need to kill the attitude of indifference toward the Word of God, kill indiscipline, and kill instability so you can pave your way to your great, God-given destiny.

I see you getting there.

Endnote

1. http://www.quotationspage.com/quote/2087.html; accessed July 3, 2012.

Conclusion

The fundamental idea behind this book is to bring you to the place where you can see and accept the fact that you are not a creation of chance; you are very strategic and significant in the plan of God. He planned every detail about you even before you were conceived, and He created you uniquely so you can bring about something not only for your family but for your generation and future generations as well. You are a child of destiny—a highly gifted and blessed person, born with much inside you to benefit humanity. You may not feel it, but you have a lot inside you to offer, and your generation is waiting for your manifestation.

Remember that in God's scheme of things, your color, race, or background is immaterial. What people think of you is immaterial. *It is what God says about you and the choices that you make that count.* Now you can choose the way of success; you can rise above your past failure and start again—you will make it if you don't give up. Now you can choose victory over defeat, courage over fear, good success over mediocrity, abundance over lack. Choose to rise and not stay down, lift your head high and do not go with your head bowed looking defeated and hopeless. The devil is a liar; there is no more limitation before you.

It is time for you to take your covenant place in destiny. You can achieve great success, you can rise above all the odds and the limitations. God will empower you to fulfill what you were created for—but you must walk with Him and give Him His place in your life and affairs. What you cannot achieve by your own power, He can help you achieve. What others cannot do for you, He can. What is impossible with people, He can make happen. With God on your side, you can fly, you can reach your full potential, you can reach your goals. Yes, you can become successful, accomplished, and influential.

I am confident you will make it!

FROM THE SAME AUTHOR

The Love of Father God

The Love of Father God unveils the heart and the never-ending love of God, the defeat and the fall of satan, and the power and the glory of the Christian faith.

As a believer, you are a new creation in Christ Jesus—the wonder of God and the miracle of Heaven. This book solves the mysteries and reveals the benefits of your role in God's Kingdom.

ISBN: 978-88-96727-31-7

I Am Who God Says I Am

People come and go, but only a few people make a meaningful impact in their lifetime. Only a few people discover their purpose, turn it into passion, and fight for it like they do not have any other option. These are the people who reach greatness.

I Am Who God Says I Am was inspired as a tool to show you that you can achieve greatness in life and that there is no limitation before you.

ISBN: 978-88-89127-94-0

Order now from Evangelista Media
Telephone: +39 085 4716623 - Fax: +39 085 9090113
Email: orders@evangelistamedia.com

Internet: www.evangelistamedia.com

Additional copies of this book and other book
titles from EVANGELISTA MEDIA™
and DESTINY IMAGE™ EUROPE
are available at your local bookstore.

We are adding new titles every month!

To view our complete catalog online, visit us at:
www.evangelistamedia.com

Follow us on Facebook
(facebook.com/EvangelistaMedia)
and Twitter (twitter.com/EM_worldwide)

Send a request for a catalog to:

**Via della Scafa, 29/14
65013 Città Sant'Angelo (Pe), ITALY
Tel. +39 085 4716623 • Fax +39 085 9090113
info@evangelistamedia.com**

"Changing the World, One Book at a Time."

Are you an author?
Do you have a "today" God-given message?

CONTACT US

We will be happy to review your manuscript
for the possibility of publication:

publisher@evangelistamedia.com
http://www.evangelistamedia.com/pages/AuthorsAppForm.htm